NATHAN GREELEY

Christian Apologetics: A Lutheran Introduction

First published by Just and Sinner 2021

First edition

ISBN: 978-1-952295-50-8

This book was professionally typeset on Reedsy.
Find out more at reedsy.com

Contents

Preface

The following short book was written to meet a perceived need for an accessible, concise, and yet relatively comprehensive introduction to apologetics aimed at a confessional Lutheran lay audience. The intention throughout was to make all the material relevant to the kinds of conversations that laypeople can expect to have with unbelieving friends, family members, and co-workers. In other words, everything was meant to be of use in personal evangelism, an activity for which there is perhaps greater need today than ever before.

Although the number of apologetic materials written by confessional Lutherans for confessional Lutherans is increasing, and many of these resources are quite accessible and practical, I do not believe one exists that not only provides a concise and easy-to-read overview of most major issues in apologetics, but also approaches these issues from a self-consciously "catholic" standpoint. By catholic standpoint, I mean an approach to apologetics that seeks to retrieve the best insights of classical Christian philosophy, as these were handed down by thinkers such as St. Augustine, St. Anselm, and St. Thomas Aquinas, and then later inherited by Lutheran scholastics such as Johann Gerhard, Abraham Calov, and Johannes Quenstedt. This patrimony is in my opinion priceless, and it should shape how Lutherans do apologetics much more than should modern philosophies, which often operate on assumptions that are antithetical to both common sense and what is best in the catholic tradition.

Though I understand that a fair number of people think of Lutheranism and the philosophy of the pre-Reformation church as being opposed, or at the least as having little to do with each other, I do not believe this is an accurate understanding of Lutheranism. For those readers who find this claim dubious, I can only encourage you to read deeply in many of the great figures of our tradition, including Melanchthon, Chemnitz, Hutter, and Gerhard, among others. Not only will you be deeply edified and led to a greater love and knowledge of our Savior, but you will also learn a great deal about true Lutheranism.

In any case, my hope for this little volume is that it will be of benefit to my fellow members of confessional Lutheran bodies, both in fortifying their own faith and in helping them to interact fruitfully with others. We live in a world in which Christianity is increasingly seen as strange, and evangelism seems ever more daunting to many. There can therefore be no such thing as too many resources for confidently engaging with this context. At the risk of sounding platitudinous, if even one person finds his or her belief in Christ or willingness to share the gospel fortified by what follows, this book will have served its purpose.

A question-and-answer format has been utilized in hopes of making the book more reader friendly and of increasing the ease with which readers can find where specific topics are addressed. The questions are numbered with two digits, the first referring to the chapter number, the second to the number of the question. Though the answers generally stand alone as responses to specific questions, there are places where knowing the answers given to previous questions will be necessary to fully comprehend what is said.

At the end of each chapter, the reader will find a list of recommended resources that are relevant to the topics discussed in that chapter. These will provide discussions that go into more depth and detail than those found in the present volume. Though they are helpful and generally support the contentions made here, they are not always in complete agreement with my own views or the doctrine of the Lutheran Confessions. They should be comprehensible for the interested lay reader, but most are more academic in tone or presentation than this book.

Many thanks must be given to Jordan Cooper for his friendship, his feedback, and the opportunity to publish this work with Just and Sinner. Likewise, thanks are due to Mark Mattes, Lisa Cooper, and Katy Cloninger for their kindness in reading and commenting on the manuscript prior to publication. Any shortcomings are of course my responsibility alone. I also must thank my wife, Anne, for her continuous support. The greatest thanks must naturally be given to the triune Lord of the universe, who alone makes all things possible. *Soli Deo Gloria!*

1

Introduction

Frank and Diana, two Christian parents, are troubled by the fact that their college-age son David seems to be drifting from the faith he was raised in. They don't feel comfortable addressing the matter with him, but they know it needs to be discussed.

Sarah wants to talk with her friend Elizabeth about Jesus, but feels unsure about how Elizabeth will react, and she's worried that Elizabeth will ask her questions she won't be able to answer.

John's brother Carl is now claiming to be an atheist, and John wants to talk to his brother about his lack of belief, but he is worried that Carl will attack the Christian beliefs they both used to share. John doesn't feel prepared for a conversation like that.

Rachel considers herself a Christian, but she has recently taken a college class that has her questioning some of the things she assumed to be true about the Bible. Now she is wondering what to believe.

All of these scenarios, and countless others like them, play out every day in real life. Virtually everyone these days has numerous friends, family members, co-workers, or acquaintances who don't believe that Christianity is true. As the Western world becomes increasingly secular, not a few Christians are finding that most of the people they interact with do not share their faith. In such an environment, it can be quite difficult to talk about or even maintain a strong faith in Christ. It is for anyone who might find themselves in circumstances like these that this book has been written. Although it consists of discussions of many issues, the overarching aim of this volume is to answer one question: Why is belief in the gospel—the promise that God will forgive contrite sinners who believe that their sins are forgiven for Christ's sake—a reasonable thing to believe? Too few Christians are confidently able to answer this question, but as the scenarios mentioned above indicate, nearly every Christian would be wise to learn how to answer it. It is my hope that the material that follows suffices to help you do that.

Achieving this purpose will require giving a basic overview of what apologetics is about and providing a guide to some effective apologetic arguments that can be used to support the claims of Christianity. My hope is that the points that follow are both simple and convincing enough that they can be usefully employed in everyday conversations with the people you interact with. Although apologetics is theoretical in its content, it is highly practical in its aim, which is to serve the church's mission of proclaiming the gospel of Jesus Christ. In this first chapter, I will introduce the subject of apologetics and discuss how best to approach using apologetic arguments.

1.1 What is apologetics?

Simply put, Christian apologetics is the part of theology occupied with the rational defense of the Christian faith. It involves making the case that Christianity is true. An apologist therefore draws on rational arguments, historical facts, and possible solutions to objections raised against Christianity in order to bring out or make clear the reasonableness of Christianity. Though it is not possible to show that Christianity is as certainly true as a necessary truth like 2 + 2 = 4, it is quite possible show that Christianity is almost certainly true. We can, for example, make it clear that God must exist and that Jesus beyond any reasonable doubt rose from the dead. The intent of this book is to give a clear presentation of how such things might be shown.

Some people think that apologetics is only for pastors, scholars, or professors. They imagine apologetics takes place mostly in books or debates between famous Christians and atheists. This, however, is not true. Apologetics is not necessarily highly academic or combative. Since the primary point of apologetics is to convince people of the truth of Christianity, it is actually much more about persuasion and inviting people to see things in a different way than it is about engaging in debates. It also happens much more often in the course of conversations between ordinary people than it does in arguments between scholars. The aim of the person doing apologetics should be simply to lead his conversation partner to realize that Christianity makes more sense of human life and the world than any competing religion or philosophy. Anyone can potentially do this if they are willing to make an effort, so both the apologist and his conversation partner can be regular, everyday people. You do not therefore need any special talents, degrees, or qualifications to use apologetics.

Because apologetics is concerned with persuading people to take Christianity seriously as a reasonable thing to believe, apologetics is a crucial tool in evangelism. This is something that is often overlooked in Lutheran circles when evangelism is discussed, but it is highly important. Many people are afraid to evangelize because they worry that they will face some question or criticism of their beliefs or claims that they will be unable to respond to or answer adequately. They wonder if they will look foolish, and whether feeble responses will only harden unbelievers in their skepticism. Apologetics, because it helps a person to know what to say in such situations, can help any believer to be more confident as he shares the gospel of Jesus Christ. Since evangelism is a duty that all Christians have, as Jesus declares in Matthew 28:19–20, there is truth in the view that knowing something about apologetics is not just a good idea. It is necessary due to the fact that it can contribute to more effective evangelism.

1.2 Are there valid objections to apologetics?

Before going further, however, it may be helpful to point out a couple of common criticisms of apologetics, and to mention why they are not really good objections. More could no doubt be mentioned, but the following two seem to be expressed most often.

The first criticism is that apologetic arguments do not actually work. The objection here is to the effectiveness of apologetics. Some people say you cannot argue someone into the faith, or that no one ever became a Christian because someone gave them an argument. A second objection, which is related to the first, is that apologetics assumes that the work of the Holy Spirit is unnecessary for conversion. This goes along with the thought that since the Holy Spirit converts hearts, there isn't really any place in Christianity for rational arguments or appeals to evidence.

Both of these objections, however, misconstrue what apologetics is all about. Regarding the latter, a biblically minded apologist does not assume that he can convert anyone without the Holy Spirit working through the word of God, or even that it is really he himself who converts anyone at all. But he does recognize that the Holy Spirit works through a variety of means to bring people to pay attention to the word, including the conversations people have with family members, friends, and co-workers. Because the Bible makes it clear that means matter in this way, and that God providentially works through believers to achieve his purposes, we can be confident that God blesses the good use of means to bring people to faith. Concerning the former objection, it is the case that many people have credited apologetic arguments with bringing them to take Christianity more seriously, and more than a few have regarded these arguments as having played an important part in their coming to know Christ. When I myself returned to Christianity as an adult after having been an agnostic for several years, apologetic arguments played a role by making me realize that I was committing myself to something real and important. Hence the claim that apologetics is entirely ineffective does not hold much water when we actually examine what real people have to say. Sometimes it might not be effective, but sometimes it is. And because it sometimes is, it is important that Christians who are involved in evangelism (which should mean all Christians) know something about it.

That all being said, it is necessary to acknowledge and understand that most people who are resistant to the Christian message do not resist it because of intellectual difficulties. It is not generally the case that they really want to become Christians, but they just cannot solve some intellectual puzzle. They might say that, but most often there is no evidence that such people have made any great effort to investigate the issue that they supposedly cannot find a solution to. The simple but unflattering truth is that most people outside of the church do not want to take on everything that Christianity involves. They do not want a new commitment that will require them to hold different values. They do not want a new commitment that will require the use of their time, energy, and treasure. They do not want a new commitment that will potentially make them unpopular or ostracized in their social circles. This is certainly understandable, given how an unbeliever sees things and what his heart loves. True Christianity requires making sacrifices with respect to worldly things. It always has and it always will. And many people, sadly, are simply not interested in making such sacrifices. The point of noting this frequent resistance to apologetics is to remind the would-be apologist that he should not be discouraged when conversations that include apologetics seem to have no effect. Intellectual issues are often not really the problem, and therefore discussing them will not have much part in the solution.

For those who do have genuine doubts and questions, however, and are on some level searching for those things that Christianity alone provides, apologetics can be invaluable. It can weaken their skepticism and encourage them to engage with God's word, through which the Holy Spirit can ignite the gift of faith in their hearts. It is in the hope of reaching people such as these that apologists practice their craft.

One additional point worth making here is that I do not think any mature Christian genuinely wants their faith to be baseless or unsupported by reasons. Some, it is true, do not want to expend the time and effort required to learn the reasons that exist, and they are tempted as a result to downplay the value of apologetics. But it is important that we not do this. Even apart from the practical usefulness of apologetics in doing evangelism and strengthening a Christian's own faith, loving God with all our mind seems to require a willingness to learn what we can about the things of God. These things include the evidence that exists for his existence and the truth of his glorious gospel.

1.3 How should Lutherans think about apologetics? Wasn't Luther against reason?

Contrary to the opinions of some, there is nothing in either Luther's writings or the broader Lutheran tradition that should make Lutherans opposed to apologetics. Luther indeed was opposed to using reason to discover the nature of human salvation or the way we can attain a relationship with God, but he was not opposed to using reason to discover truths about the world around us or to explore the facts of history. Apologetics, as understood by many, is chiefly concerned with these latter things. It is concerned, in other words, with the twin truths that the natural world bears witness to the reality of God and that the facts of history support the truth of the Christian revelation.

We should also remember that Luther's sixteenth-century world was a very different one than ours. Virtually everyone he knew had been baptized and raised in a deeply Christian setting. If it seems that Luther did not pay much attention to apologetic arguments for things like the existence of God or the reliability of the Bible, we should not take that to mean that he would give little attention to such matters in different circumstances. A more plausible view is that in his context, giving attention to these matters was simply unnecessary, and thus he was not occupied with them. When circumstances changed, and our culture began to noticeably lose its Christian moorings, later Lutherans with increasing frequency did become engaged in apologetics. In the nineteenth century, a conservative Lutheran named Christoph Ernst Luthardt (1823–1902) wrote extensively on apologetic issues. Another Lutheran theologian, Theodore Graebner (1876–1950), wrote a large and important work in the first half of the twentieth century criticizing atheism and the view that only matter exists. And in recent times, one of the most influential apologists in the world has been a confessional Lutheran, namely John Warwick Montgomery (1931–).

You might wonder if Lutheran theology would require Lutherans to use a unique or specific kind of apologetics, such as an approach that focuses on certain kinds of arguments or evangelism strategies. In the Reformed tradition, for example, some people hold that the doctrines of original sin and total depravity rule out any apologetic arguments that require the belief that unregenerate people and regenerate people share some common assumptions. I myself do not believe the Lutheran tradition requires any particular kind of apologetics, nor is it the case that Lutherans generally regard any variety of apologetic arguments as "off limits." However, I do think it is wise to avoid any type of apologetics that seems to depend on counterintuitive or distinctively modern assumptions. The aforementioned Reformed believers sometimes presume there are no meaningful facts apart from their subjective reception by interpreters, which is a distinctively modern (some might say postmodern) way of thinking. On such a view, what something means cannot be inherent to it, or truly objective. Because they adopt this view, these Reformed Christians try to avoid arguments that appeal to objective facts. If we were to do this, however, we would be cutting ourselves off from the collective wisdom of the church throughout the ages, since traditionally the church has always affirmed the objectivity of facts in making apologetic arguments. What all this entails is that Lutherans should be willing to learn from any Christian apologists, at least to the extent that they are not holding positions that are inimical to historic Christianity.

Of course, when talking about why Christians should be Lutheran, a different kind of apologetics will be necessary. Whereas an apologetic directed to non-believers will not presuppose the truth of the Bible, but will argue for it, an apologetic case for Lutheranism will be primarily based on arguments that assume that the Bible is true and in fact inerrant. Taking this view as a starting point, such an apologetic argument will make the case that Lutheran doctrine alone accords with the correct meaning of the Bible. Though in this book we will be chiefly concerned with the kinds of arguments that can be used to defend fundamental beliefs like the reality of God, the resurrection of Christ, and the trustworthiness of the Bible, some attention will be given in the final chapter to the question of why a Christian should be Lutheran.

1.4 Are there any preconditions of doing apologetics?

You might wonder if there is anything a person should know before getting started with apologetics. It should be mentioned in this connection that to employ apologetics effectively, there must be certain common assumptions that both parties in a conversation share. There can be no persuasion if there are not, to begin with, some truths and values held in common. This is because without some common ground, there is nothing to appeal to in making an argument. Hence, if it were possible for two people to truly disagree about everything, then there would not be any way that one of them could persuade the other of anything. Thankfully, human beings are similar enough that virtually everybody who is sane and has reached a certain level of maturity shares many basic convictions with most other people. This is true even between regenerate Christians and unbelievers. As a result, fruitful debate and discussion with those who disagree with us is often possible, even though it might prove difficult, at least initially.

Among these shared principles, a few should be pointed out. First, let us consider the principles of logic. Everyone will agree that a statement cannot be true and false at the same time in the exact same sense. They will concur in affirming that either a statement or its denial must be true. Everyone will likewise agree that some things are true by definition: a part cannot be greater than the whole, nor can a bachelor be married. Other shared beliefs are metaphysical or ethical principles that we seem to intuitively grasp. These include the belief that everything that begins to exist must have a cause capable of producing it, that there is an external world outside of human minds, that design necessarily implies a designer, and that people have a duty to do good and avoid evil.

On the basis of assumptions such as these, a wide range of apologetic arguments can be successfully developed, as we will see in the remainder of this book. Although some of these assumptions are occasionally denied in theory, or in the course of debate, they are almost never denied in practice, and practice is the key to determining what someone really believes. The apologist should not hesitate to point out if there seems to be a tension between what someone claims and what they do, for this is one of the chief ways in which people are pushed to reflect on the truth of their assertions. For example, if someone claims that the universe may have begun to exist without any cause or reason, you can point out that they never seem to think this could be the case with respect to anything else.

Other than understanding the importance of these widespread convictions, the only thing necessary for effective apologetic conversations is that the people involved be willing to think carefully and examine their beliefs with the goal of seeking the truth. This condition is often not met, but we should not be discouraged in such cases, for sometimes the Holy Spirit will use what is said during a conversation to change a heart and mind at a much later time.

One other thing worth mentioning here is how important it is that the apologist approach discussions with others in the right spirit. First Peter 3:15 commands us to give a reason for the hope that is in us, but to do it with gentleness and respect. We therefore have to engage in apologetics out of genuine concern for the people we are talking to, and not simply out of a wish to show off our knowledge or to win an argument. If the argument is won but the person is lost, nothing of great significance has been gained.

1.5 What is the first step when actually doing apologetics?

The first thing you should do will probably already have begun to happen before you even form an intention to use apologetics. It is to get to know your audience or conversation partners. This can be done in both a general and a particular sense. In a general sense, you should try to understand the culture in which you live and witness, since everyone is influenced by their cultural context, at least to some extent. Most people are influenced by it much more than they realize. Arriving at such an understanding will involve attaining a knowledge of the attitudes and beliefs that are prevalent in the areas in which you live and work. It will also mean understanding where these views originally came from and why many people find them believable. Everyone knows we live in a society that is vastly different now than it was a century or even a half century ago. Beliefs that seemed obvious and were taken for granted by our great-grandparents often seem bizarre and even harmful to people today, and people today believe things our great-grandparents would have been shocked by. Having a grasp of what has changed and why it has changed will help a Christian of today to see how best to approach certain issues. It will help him to discern what the best responses are to objections and questions from unbelievers. Later in this book, we will look at several things unbelievers often say today in response to the Christian message.

In a particular sense, you should also find out about the personal stories of the people with whom you are talking. This includes learning what their religious background is, what judgments they have formed about Christianity, and what reasons they might give for not being a Christian. You should also see if they have any questions about Christianity that they do not think have been adequately answered. Sometimes it will take time to find out such things without prying or seeming nosy, so patience can be important. But it is necessary in any case that we get a sense of whom we are talking with, for in order to say something meaningful and helpful, we naturally have to know the mindset, beliefs, and feelings of the people we are talking with. People are also much more likely to listen to someone who they think knows them well and cares about them, so getting to know people is crucial for multiple reasons. If we look at our own lives, our biggest influences usually have been people with whom we have had a significant personal connection.

Based on what you learn about a conversation partner, you can then make appropriate decisions about how to use apologetics. Some people will want plausible answers to specific questions. Some people will need to be gently corrected because they will have misconceptions about Christianity. Others will be so antagonistic to Christianity, and so unwilling to listen to any talk in its favor, that you will only be able to pray for them, not reason with them. The many arguments and answers that are discussed in this book will hopefully be helpful in crafting a customized response that can speak to people wherever they are on the spectrum. You can regard these arguments and responses as items in a toolkit that can be employed as the situation demands. When doing apologetics, it is always important to adapt to the situation.

1.6 What is an apologetic method?

One other matter that perhaps should be addressed in this first chapter is the issue of apologetic methodology. A method, of course, is simply a well-thought-out way of doing something, and an apologetic method is therefore a well-thought-out way of approaching apologetics. There are a few different methods out there, and they have different ideas about what kinds of arguments are helpful and what a person should focus on in making a case for Christianity. This being the case, it will be helpful to briefly review them and indicate the method that is employed in this book.

Some people, as already mentioned, do not see much value or need for apologetics. We can call such people fideists, because they think faith does not need and perhaps cannot really acquire any support from reason or evidence. This is not so much an apologetic method, then, as the rejection of any such method. There is a grain of truth in fideism, in that faith is a supernatural gift, and as such, it will never have its true source in apologetic arguments. But it is also true that faith is only created in contexts where the word of God can be read or heard and attentively listened to. Since apologetics can and often does play a key role in creating such contexts for individuals and groups of people, it is important and necessary. Because of this, there is no reason to recommend fideistic thinking. An honest appraisal of the facts will lead any person to admit that not only have many people been led to Christ through considering the evidence for Christianity, but many also have left Christianity because they were under the impression that it was no more plausible than myths and legends. Dispensing with apologetics should therefore not be regarded as a real option.

Perhaps the most common methodological view in the history of the church is what is often called classical apologetics. Classical apologetics insists that the first and most fundamental apologetic issue is the question of God's reality. Therefore, the classical apologist will seek to employ arguments that show that God exists, or at least is highly likely to exist. After a case for God's existence is made, the apologist will then seek to mount a defense of the truth of the Bible and the fact that Jesus really rose from the dead and was who he claimed to be, namely, the divine Son of God.

Classical apologetics is closely tied to a traditional distinction between natural and special revelation. Natural revelation is all the knowledge of God that is revealed or has the potential to be revealed through nature, including by means of the exercise of human reason. Special revelation is a knowledge of God that is obtained through God's granting of information to specific people in particular times and places. Both of these types of revelation are regarded as real in the Bible. You can consult, for example, Psalm 19 or Romans 1 to see the Bible unequivocally affirming the reality of natural revelation. The method of classical apologetics first calls attention to this natural revelation and points out the ways in which the natural world reveals God's reality to us. It then brings to light the reasons we have for believing in the special revelation that is found in the Bible. Though confidence in the complete truth of Scripture can only be a gift provided by the Holy Spirit working in our hearts, the evidence mustered by the apologist can lead people to pay heed to the word and thus can provide an opportunity for the Spirit to do this marvelous work.

Another method is typically referred to as evidential apologetics. This view of what apologetics involves is quite similar to classical apologetics, in that it places high value on reasons and facts. Most evidential apologists are also appreciative of theistic arguments. Evidentialism differs, however, in that it denies that proving the existence of God is a necessary element in providing an apologetic case for Christianity. On this view, if a person can prove that the Bible is reliable and that Christ rose from the dead, then this is sufficient to vouch for both God's existence and the truth of Christianity.

Yet another perspective is what is known as presuppositionalism. This is a quite different understanding of apologetics from all of those already mentioned. It has its origins in Reformed Christianity and borrows some of its key assumptions from modern philosophy. We have already touched on some of its tenets when discussing the question of whether or not Lutherans should use a particular approach to apologetics. The presuppositionalist believes that there is no way to prove the truth of Christianity to an unbeliever, since such a person has an entirely different worldview and will never accept the assumptions that arguments for Christianity are based upon. The unbeliever will deny that there is any natural revelation and will resist the evidence for special revelation. All an apologist can do, then, according to the presuppositionalist, is point to the fact that the unbeliever's own beliefs are inconsistent or incoherent. This may push the unbeliever to accept Christianity, which comprises the only consistent set of beliefs.

One final way of doing apologetics that I will mention is to focus on how Christianity may provide benefits to believers, whether in this life or the life to come. We can call this a pragmatic apologetic. It does not employ or defend either special or general revelation. This view argues instead that those who believe possibly stand to gain something that those who do not believe will necessarily miss out on. Therefore, belief is more rational than unbelief.

It is my view that the best apologetic method is the classical one. It is the method that seems to best grasp what is needed in the doing of apologetics, and it has the most realistic goals. It corresponds to the two types of revelation that are clearly set forth in the Scriptures, that from nature and that from God's special acts in history. Evidential apologetics seems to miss an important factor in overlooking the importance of arguments for God's existence and what we can discover through God's natural revelation. Presuppositionalism is unrealistic in that it seems to require that all other worldviews can be exhaustively and impartially examined, and that Christianity can itself be shown to be entirely consistent from a human point of view. Pragmatic apologetics is inadequate because such an approach must simply assume without sufficient warrant that Christianity will provide more benefits than any other possible religion or philosophy. This leaves classical apologetics as the best of the available options. As such, in what follows, we will operate on the assumption that the classical method is the best and most useful for persuading unbelievers to take Christianity seriously.

In the next chapter, we will look at the history of how apologetics has been used in the church. This will help us to provide some background for everything else that will be discussed later in the book.

For Further Reading

Becker, Siegbert W. *The Foolishness of God: The Place of Reason in the Theology of Martin Luther*. Milwaukee: Northwestern Publishing, 1982.

Cooper, Jordan. *Prolegomena: A Defense of the Scholastic Method*. Ithaca, NY: Just and Sinner, 2020.

Gerrish, B. A. *Grace and Reason: A Study in the Theology of Luther*. Eugene, OR: Wipf and Stock, 2005.

Guinness, Os. *Fool's Talk: Recovering the Art of Christian Persuasion*. Downers Grove, IL: InterVarsity, 2015.

Mattes, Mark C. "A Lutheran Case for Apologetics." In *Law and Gospel in Action: Foundations, Ethics, Church*. Irvine, CA: 1517 Publishing, 2018.

Montgomery, John Warwick. *Defending the Gospel in Legal Style: Essays on Legal Apologetics & the Justification of Classical Christian Faith*. Eugene, OR: Wipf and Stock, 2017.

Morley, Brian K. *Mapping Apologetics: Comparing Contemporary Approaches*. Downers Grove, IL: 2015.

Sproul, R. C., John Gerstner, and Arthur Lindsley. *Classical Apologetics: A Rational Defense of the Christian Faith and Critique of Presuppositional Apologetics*. Grand Rapids, MI: Zondervan Academic, 1984.

2

The History of Apologetics

Since apologetics is, as pointed out in the previous chapter, closely connected with evangelism, it might be asked why having a knowledge of the history of apologetics is of value. Many books on apologetics in fact pay little, if any, attention to it, which might make it seem unimportant or of no use. But to think this would be a mistake. By knowing something about how apologetics was done in the past, we can gain a sense of how different objections to Christianity developed and how responses to these were developed in turn. This will make us more aware of how difficult objections actually are to address and more confident about the adequacy of our responses.

Sometimes people will assume that they are the first person to have thought of a particular objection to Christianity, or that the church has no answer to an objection because they themselves have never encountered one. Having such thoughts is almost always the result of not knowing much at all about the history of apologetics. The truth is that there is not a single reasonable objection that has not been carefully considered and answered by someone at some time. Many well-known difficulties have been addressed by brilliant philosophers and theologians countless times. Knowing something about the history of apologetics can therefore give us assurance that although we might not always have a good answer to every question, a fellow believer in the past probably has had a good response.

Though it is impossible to here treat the history of apologetics in a comprehensive manner, it will be useful and hopefully informative to mention some of the key emphases that can be found in apologetic works from different eras of the history of the church.

2.1 When did Christian apologetics begin?

The first Christian apologists were the apostles themselves. This is not surprising, because, as mentioned previously, apologetics is intimately connected to evangelism. Since the apostles were constantly engaged in evangelism towards an often hostile and skeptical audience, doing apologetics was an essential part of their mission.

We get a clear picture of what an apostle's apologetics looked like in the Bible itself. In Acts 17, we read about the apostle Paul's encounter with pagans in Athens. Athens was renowned throughout the world at that time as a center of learning and philosophy. That being the case, Paul no doubt expected to find some intellectuals there who would be eager to challenge his message.

There are some important things that Paul does in Acts 17 that are worth pointing out. First, he looks for things that he has in common with his audience. Both Paul and his listeners believe that God exists; the question is, who is this God and what can we know about him? Paul points out that the God he is talking about is the God who created the world and now provides for it. He adds that since this God made us, beings who have minds, it makes no sense to identify God with anything made of matter. Nothing that lacks a mind could possibly make something that has a mind. At this point, Paul has clearly shown to those listening to his speech that the creator God cannot therefore be identified with any of the idols made of metal, stone, or wood that were prevalent among them. Paul then tells his listeners that the creator demands that everyone repent, because he will judge the world through a man that he has chosen to be the judge of the world. This has been proven, Paul adds, because this man was raised from the dead.

We see here in a basic form the method of classical apologetics. First, God's reality is argued for. Although the Athenians are believers in many gods, including an "Unknown God" to whom they have erected an altar, they do not know who this God is or what he is like. Paul makes it clear that the God who created the world and human spirits cannot be anything but a spirit. He then goes on to argue that this God has been active in human history and has furnished proof of this by raising a man, namely Jesus, from the dead. Hence, we see both a clarification of who God is, by using natural revelation, and then a claim made about what God's will is and what he has done in human history, which comes from special revelation. As was discussed in the previous chapter, moving in this way from arguments founded on natural revelation to arguments based on special revelation is generally the best way to proceed in apologetic conversations.

2.2 What did apologetics look like in the early church?

In the early centuries of the church, we can be sure that similar methods of persuasion as found in Paul's speech in Athens were also employed by other Christians in the course of everyday evangelism. The first written works devoted specifically to apologetics were written in the second century A.D. In these writings, Christian apologists sought to respond to some of the false and slanderous claims being made about Christianity by pagans. The works were therefore primarily defensive, in that they were not trying to show that paganism was false, but were trying to make it clear that Christianity was not something that upstanding and fair-minded people in the Roman Empire should despise or oppose.

The early church also inaugurated an interest in how philosophy (knowledge about the world, God, and man that can be obtained through reason or natural revelation) should be related to theology (knowledge of these things that is revealed in the Scriptures). This then became a matter of lasting concern throughout the history of Christianity. Although we cannot generalize too much, it can be said that the early church fathers, with few exceptions, were interested in and saw value in Greek and Roman philosophy, particularly the schools of the Platonists and the Stoics. They acknowledged that pagan philosophy was marked by many errors, but held that the truths found in it could nonetheless corroborate and aid in the understanding of revealed theology.

One of the most significant apologists in the early centuries of the church was St. Justin Martyr (ca. 100–ca. 165). Justin, a pagan Platonist philosopher who converted to Christianity, wrote three significant apologetic works. One of the major themes of his writings is that nothing in Christianity promotes immorality or wrongdoing, and therefore no one should be punished simply for being Christian. Another theme is that the knowledge provided by Christianity completes and perfects whatever truth was known to pagans apart from Christ. We also find in Justin's apologetic works descriptions of Christian practices. This was important so that pagan critics did not misunderstand or falsely characterize the things that Christians did. One more important feature of Justin's apologetics was his calling attention to prophecies found in the Old Testament that were fulfilled by Christ.

Another representative apologist of the second century was Athenagoras of Athens (ca. 133–ca. 190). Like Justin, he was a pagan philosopher who converted to Christianity. There are two significant apologetic works that he authored. In one of these, he discusses similar issues to those raised by Justin. In the other, he argues for the doctrine of bodily resurrection, and shows that it is not opposed to reason. This was important in his context, because pagan philosophers only believed at most that the soul could be immortal. The notion that a body might be revivified would have struck them as absurd.

After Christianity became an officially recognized religion of the Roman Empire in the fourth century, apologetic arguments asserting that Christianity should be tolerated were no longer necessary. But there were still pagan intellectuals in the Roman Empire, and this being the case, there was still a need to convince them of the truth of Christianity. Arguably the greatest of the church fathers, St. Augustine (354–430), was also an important philosopher and apologist to these pagans. Not only did he argue in several of his writings that man can only be satisfied by knowing the God revealed in Christ, but he also made a vigorous case against the credibility of Roman paganism in one of his greatest works, *The City of God*. In Augustine we also find arguments for the existence of God and the reality of the soul, two important matters that are of perennial concern to apologists.

2.3 What did apologetics look like in the medieval church?

In medieval Europe, most Christians had relatively little contact with unbelievers. This was especially true in rural areas. The pagan Greco-Roman culture of the ancient world was long past. Christianity was everywhere, and although a fair number of people lived lives worthy of reproach, few people baptized into the church were willing to openly disagree or express skepticism about established Christian doctrines. Almost no one at this time would have admitted to being an atheist.

The ubiquity of Christianity during this age did not mean, however, that apologetic works and writings relevant to apologetics became uncommon. One reason for this is that Christians maintained a keen awareness that Jews resided among them, and that Muslims dwelled in great numbers beyond the borders of Christendom. Another factor is that the relationship of philosophy to theology remained of immense interest during this period. Theologians were also attempting during this time to systematize Christian doctrine on an unprecedented scale, and in doing so, they had to achieve further clarity about the role reason should play in relation to revealed theology. All of these concerns meant that arguments of use in apologetics were a frequent topic of discussion.

One of the most significant figures in the discussion of apologetics in the Middle Ages was St. Anselm of Canterbury (ca. 1033–1109). St. Anselm, like virtually all early medieval theologians in western Europe, was highly influenced by St. Augustine. Though he did not write any works that were specifically intended to convince unbelievers of the truth of Christianity, virtually everything he wrote is of interest to apologists, because his writings are full of sharp reasoning and well-constructed arguments. Though his claim to fame is that he developed a new argument for the existence of God (now referred to as the ontological argument), it is arguably his view of the nature of theology that was his most important contribution. For Anselm, theology was the practice of faith seeking understanding, or of seeking to see the reasons behind, and the connections between, various doctrines.

Another medieval thinker of even more importance than Anselm was St. Thomas Aquinas (1225–1274). Aquinas wrote a massive work that was clearly intended to be an apologetic case for Christianity. Its Latin title is *Summa Contra Gentiles*. It appears his hope was that this work would be used by Christians in Spain and elsewhere in their interactions with Jews and Muslims. In this work and others, Aquinas put forward several arguments for the existence of God that are of great interest, even today. We will examine some of them in the next chapter.

Like most theologians of this time, Aquinas was also interested in the question of the relationship of philosophy to theology. In the beginning of another one of his major works, his *Summa Theologiae,* he articulated a view of this relationship that remains popular today. He held that certain truths can be discovered by reason alone, while others can be discovered by revelation alone. A third group can be learned in both ways. Truths that can be discovered by reason operating on its own belong to the discipline of philosophy. Truths that can only be discovered by revelation belong to the domain of theology. Truths that can be learned by means of both can be the subject of both. He also held that truths in philosophy cannot contradict those in theology, and that even though philosophy is able to discover truths on its own, any philosophical view must be regarded as mistaken if it contradicts God's revelation in Scripture. Hence, philosophy is in a sense independent from theology, but it is still subject to the oversight of theology.

2.4 What happened to apologetics after the Reformation?

During the century following the Reformation, apologetic arguments for Christianity were neglected in favor of arguments presented in support of the doctrines of specific Christian confessions. This is unsurprising, as the chief concern at this time was not with the truth of Christianity broadly speaking, but with the right way to understand specific doctrines, and with which rival confession was correct in its understanding. This is not to say, however, that nothing at all was written that was pertinent to apologetics in a broad sense. In the Lutheran tradition, Philipp Melanchthon (1497–1560) kept an interest in classical philosophy alive, and in his works he reiterated several arguments for God's existence. This attention given to such arguments was maintained in the writings of later Lutherans, such as Jakob Heerbrand (1521–1600), Leonhard Hutter (1563–1616), and Johann Gerhard (1582–1637). For these figures, the main purpose of theistic proofs was not to convince people who did not believe in the reality of God, for such people were still exceedingly rare. It was rather to strengthen the faith of those who already believed. Such arguments also were considered an important thing to include when writing systematic theological works, since they were important elements of any complete treatment of the doctrine of God.

With the onset of the Enlightenment in the later years of the seventeenth century, the need for apologetics aimed at unbelievers once again became pressing. This was a period of growing skepticism and irreligion. Reason was often assumed to be a better guide to truth than revelation. Unfortunately, the influence of these changes was so pervasive that even many apologists trying to defend the faith were not themselves entirely committed to sound doctrine. One such apologist was Gottfried Wilhelm Leibniz (1646–1716), who was a Lutheran and appears to have had a sincere faith but was not confessional in any sense. In any case, Leibniz made several contributions to apologetics, including impressive formulations of classical arguments for the existence of God and a groundbreaking attempt to solve the problem of why God permits evil.

As the Enlightenment progressed, deism became increasingly popular. This view is the belief that a God exists, but that he has not revealed himself to any particular people at any particular time and place. It thus denies all special revelation, along with all the miracles and providential events related in the Bible. Deists typically held that people would be accepted by God as long as they were "good" people. Christ was perhaps an admirable teacher, but nothing more. Several deists wrote books devoted to arguing that the Bible is unreliable in order to support their view that Christ and his righteousness are unnecessary for salvation. In response, many eighteenth-century theologians and philosophers worked to refute the claims of deism.

One prominent English opponent of this movement was Thomas Sherlock (1678–1761). Sherlock wrote an important work that assessed the credibility of the witnesses to Jesus' resurrection. On the basis of the evident facts of Jesus' life and the lives of his first followers, he asserted that it would be highly unreasonable to charge that stories of his resurrection were made up. Sherlock's work was very popular and went through over a dozen editions. The most famous critic of the deists' distrust of revealed religion, however, was another Englishman named Joseph Butler (1692–1752). Butler, in his *Analogy of Religion, Natural and Revealed, to the Constitution and Course of Nature,* took a different approach than Sherlock. Butler argued that there are enough similarities between our knowledge of the natural world and the Christian revelation that in the interest of consistency, the deists should accept the latter if they accept the former. He also claimed that the sheer number of miracles and fulfilled prophecies found in the histories of the Jews and the Christians makes it highly probable that such miracles and prophecies truly occurred.

In the nineteenth century, the type of apologetic found in Sherlock was reiterated by an American law professor named Simon Greenleaf (1783–1853). Greenleaf's contribution to apologetics is found in his *Testimony of the Evangelists, Examined by the Rules of Evidence Administered in Courts of Justice*. In this book, Greenleaf attempted to show that according to legal criteria, the four canonical Gospels meet every reasonable requirement for being judged trustworthy, and therefore that Christianity is worthy of belief.

In the decades after Greenleaf's death, the skepticism of the Enlightenment only deepened in many circles. It became common for worldly people, especially in scientific, academic, and literary circles, to profess agnosticism about the reality of God. The latter half of the nineteenth century saw a major challenge to orthodox Christianity in the form of Darwinian evolutionary theory. Charles Darwin, an English scientist, began his career with a rather tepid belief in God, but by the end of his life, he had become an agnostic under the influence of his own theory, which taught that the various species on earth have emerged through purely random processes. A notable early opponent of his theory was Charles Hodge (1797–1878), a professor at Princeton Theological Seminary. Hodge argued that Darwinism is really a form of atheism because it denies all purpose in the natural world. Moreover, he insisted that it was highly implausible and only favored by those who were unbelievers and were therefore looking to establish an explanation of life that made no reference to God.

2.5 What has happened regarding apologetics in recent times?

During the twentieth century, opposition to Christianity became commonplace among cultural elites, and in most mainline Christian denominations, traditional views were often attacked. Darwin's theory and a naturalist view of reality (one which assumes there is nothing truly supernatural) were both often taken for granted. Though critics of Christianity held a variety of views and often differed with each other, they were generally united in thinking that traditional forms of Christianity could no longer be believed by thoughtful people.

In this context, several able apologists arose who made strong cases for the truth of classic tenets of the Christian faith. In fact, it seems true that apologetics as a field of inquiry only became more accomplished and impressive during this period as opposition to Christianity increased. The more common attacks became, the stronger the defenses grew. We can thank God that through his providence he saw fit to raise up many people who were capable defenders of the truth of our faith.

The most esteemed twentieth-century apologist was the Englishman C. S. Lewis (1898–1963), an atheist who converted to Christianity. Lewis in many works sought to draw out the ways in which Christianity makes sense of the world and human life. He did this through a wide variety of writings, from essays and scholarly works to fictional books for children. Many people today regard him as among the most insightful and wise thinkers in the history of the Christian church.

Another major twentieth-century apologist, mentioned already in this book, was John Warwick Montgomery (1931–), a convert to confessional Lutheranism. Montgomery worked primarily in the tradition of Sherlock and Greenleaf, in that he attempted to show how a fair-minded appraisal of the historical facts relevant to Christianity should lead to a verdict in its favor.

Today many people are continuing to do excellent work in the area of apologetics. It should be noted, however, that those apologists who receive the most attention in the world of Evangelical Christianity are not always entirely sound from a theological standpoint. They sometimes hold novel views about the nature of God, the incarnation, and other doctrines. Hence it is important to approach apologetic works coming out of Evangelicalism with some caution. A recent Roman Catholic figure who has written several excellent books that are highly relevant to doing apologetics and which are generally free from such problems is Edward Feser (1968–). Feser has sought to show how the thought of St. Thomas Aquinas continues to be relevant and suitable for doing apologetics and philosophy. His work happens to coincide with a recent revival of interest in Aquinas' ideas among many Protestants. Such Protestants believe that Aquinas managed to develop a compelling Christian philosophy that successfully synthesized biblical truth with the best insights of ancient philosophy. For those who share this view, the great medieval thinker remains of more use to biblically faithful Christians today than virtually any philosopher since his time.

Following this highly abbreviated but hopefully helpful summary of some of the key developments and figures in the history of Christian apologetics, and this assessment of where things stand today, in the next chapter we will look at arguments for the conclusion that God exists.

For Further Reading

Clifford, Ross. *John Warwick Montgomery's Legal Apologetic: An Apologetic for All Seasons*. Eugene, OR: Wipf and Stock, 2016.

Davies, Brian. *Thomas Aquinas's Summa Contra Gentiles: A Guide and Commentary*. Oxford: Oxford University Press, 2016.

Dulles, Avery. *A History of Apologetics*. San Francisco: Ignatius Press, 2005.

Feser, Edward. *Aquinas: A Beginner's Guide*. Oxford: Oneworld, 2009.

Forrest, Benjamin K., Joshua D. Chatraw, and Alister E. McGrath, eds. *The History of Apologetics: A Biographical and Methodological Introduction*. Grand Rapids, MI: Zondervan Academic, 2020.

Gilson, Etienne. *History of Christian Philosophy in the Middle Ages*. Washington D.C.: Catholic University of America Press, 2019.

_____. *The Spirit of Medieval Philosophy*. Notre Dame, IN: University of Notre Dame Press, 1991.

MacSwain, Robert, and Michael Swain, eds. *The Cambridge Companion to C. S. Lewis*. Cambridge: Cambridge University Press, 2010.

Pettersen, Alvyn. *Second-Century Apologists*. Eugene, OR: Cascade, 2020.

TeSelle, Eugene. *Augustine's Strategy as an Apologist*. Eugene, OR: Wipf and Stock, 2010.

3

Arguments for God's Existence

In orthodox Lutheranism, it has generally been held that all human beings have an innate knowledge of God as their creator and lawgiver. This knowledge, however, can be, and inevitably is, suppressed or distorted by people in our fallen state. Because of this, it can be useful to employ rational arguments that prove the existence of God, so that people might be reminded of what they on some level are already implicitly aware of. Though many today (unfortunately even inside the church) are skeptical about the possibility of demonstrating God's reality, the historic mainstream of Christianity has always held that it is possible to show by means of rational arguments that God must exist. In what follows, we will examine several arguments that have a distinguished place in the history of apologetics. Each of them is in my opinion sufficient to show that there is a God, and, taken together, they amount to an exceedingly strong case for his reality.

3.1 What is needed for a good argument for God's existence?

There are several broad types of arguments for God's existence, and within these types there are a great number of specific formulations that differ in slight ways from each other. A good argument for God's existence, like a good argument of any kind, will be both valid and sound. Any argument will be based on beliefs or assertions that function as the "premises" of the argument. A valid argument is one that takes these premises and organizes them in such a way that a specific conclusion logically follows. A sound argument will be valid, but will have the additional virtue of having premises that are true. A convincing argument will be one that appears either sound or probably sound. Validity and soundness, however, are not the only aspects of arguments that matter. It is also advantageous when arguments are simple and can be easily understood, because arguments of this kind will appear more forceful and thus will be more likely to convince people of the truth of their conclusions. If an argument is extremely simple, however, it will quite possibly be lacking in validity or soundness, so it is important that one of these things not be sacrificed for the sake of another.

It is necessary to keep in mind that a good argument need not be one that gains everyone's assent to its conclusion. For in fact no argument for any important conclusion about reality ever succeeds in doing this. No premise in any such argument is ever accepted by everyone without exception. Rather, a good argument should be defined simply as one that has no obvious problems because it appears sound, is clearly valid, and is found convincing by many people who have carefully considered it. This is the best one can hope for when it comes to arguments for God's existence. That might disappoint some who would like to have an argument that no unbeliever could possibly reject or resist, but it is certainly sufficient to establish that belief in God is entirely rational.

3.2 What types or categories of arguments are there?

There is no classification of arguments that is accepted by everyone. However, I can mention some major types that are often discussed. One includes arguments that begin from some element of human experience. These are often called *a posteriori* arguments, because they rely on our knowledge of things that we obtain after or by means of experience. There are a variety of arguments that fall under this category. A well-known example is a group of arguments called cosmological arguments. These arguments take as their starting point observations about general features of the world and then argue that God must exist to explain or account for these features. Another type of *a posteriori* argument that is perennially popular is the category of teleological arguments. These arguments look at particular things in the world and argue that they show signs of being designed or directed for the sake of specific purposes. The only plausible source of this design, according to these arguments, is an intelligent creator. Moral arguments look at the existence of moral truths or obligations, of our certainty that people ought to do what is right and avoid what is wrong. They reason that these things can only be objectively true and real in the way we take them to be if God exists. There are also other less commonly encountered *a posteriori* arguments, some of which will be discussed later, such as the argument from eternal truths and the argument from desire.

Another broad category consists of arguments that reason not from aspects of our experience of the world, but from abstract concepts or ideas. These are commonly called *a priori* arguments, because they do not depend on our knowledge of the world. They can thus be employed prior to experience, at least in principle. The most famous argument of this kind is the ontological argument, which argues that the very idea of God or a perfect being shows that it is necessary that he exists.

One final overarching category that I will mention involves pragmatic or existential arguments. These argue not that God exists, but that belief in him can be justified, at least in some situations, because it is in our best interest to believe. In this category would fall Pascal's Wager, a famous argument that essentially argues that the believer has nothing to lose and everything to gain by putting faith in God, while the unbeliever has everything to lose and nothing significant to gain by rejecting faith in him.

Which arguments are best or most helpful is a question that receives various answers. My own view is that *a posteriori* arguments are generally the most convincing and therefore of the greatest use in conversations with skeptics and unbelievers. The ontological argument can be difficult to understand, and even when understood and presented in a valid form, its soundness is often unclear, since it must assume that the idea of a perfect being is completely free from contradiction. Pragmatic arguments tend to prove too much, in that pragmatic reasoning could be employed to justify any kind of belief that seems to provide some sort of real or imagined benefit. Given the limitations of these latter two types of arguments, in what follows, the types of *a posteriori* arguments mentioned above will be the objects of our attention.

3.3 How does a cosmological argument work?

Cosmological arguments, as mentioned above, typically begin by noting some general feature of the universe. One feature commonly focused on is the reality of change; another is causality. Yet a third is contingency, or the existence of things that could possibly either exist or not exist. Cosmological arguments also take into consideration and employ commonsense principles such as that nothing can be the cause of itself, everything that begins to exist must have a cause, and causes must be able or adequate to explain their effects. These principles cannot be proven, because they are just as obviously true as any principle that could be used to support them. They therefore must be assumed to be true. Yet this is not a weakness of this type of argument, for these assumptions appear to be ones that humans have to take for granted and by nature do take for granted. They also appear to be true without exception in our experience. If someone refuses to affirm them when discussing arguments for God's existence, it is perfectly legitimate to point out that he seems to accept them with respect to all other matters. As will be seen in greater detail in what follows, when these commonsense assumptions are applied to the general features of the universe mentioned above, we find ourselves driven to admit the existence of God.

3.4 What is the argument from motion?

The argument from motion is presented in its most well-known formulation by Thomas Aquinas, who discusses it both in his *Summa Contra Gentiles* and *Summa Theologiae*. The argument was also employed by the Lutheran Johann Gerhard, who was mentioned in the previous chapter. Gerhard's version of the argument has essentially the same form that it takes in Aquinas. This is unsurprising, because it is clear that Gerhard was highly familiar with and appreciative of Aquinas' writings. Gerhard writes:

> By our sense we perceive that some things in this world move. Moreover, everything that moves must be moved by something else because nothing can be at the same time actual and potential with reference to the same thing. But in the things that move and are moved, there is no progression to infinity because there would be no first mover nor, as a consequence, would there be anything else, because secondary moving things do not move except through that which is from the first motion. It is necessary, then, to arrive at one first mover, whom we call "God." (*ONGT*, 60)

Understanding the significance of what Gerhard asserts here will require some explanation. First, it is important to understand that when the word *motion* is used, really any kind of change is meant. Hence the argument begins by simply noting that we observe changes in the world. It then claims that everything that changes must be changed by something else. This may not seem obviously true. For example, the heart of an animal moves its own blood. Doesn't this mean that the change the animal undergoes is self-caused? The answer is no, at least not in a strict sense. The heart and the blood are two distinct things. The assertion being made then is that nothing that is absolutely the same can change itself.

The concepts of actuality and potentiality are next introduced to help explain why this is the case. These concepts come from the philosophy of Aristotle, but they have been used by many Christian theologians, including, most notably, Aquinas. To truly grasp the power of this argument, the meaning of these concepts and how they reflect reality must be understood.

Actuality is a property possessed by everything that really exists. This is contrasted with potentiality, which is the possibility that something has to become actual based on what is already actual. All created things, at least while they exist, are a mixture of actuality and potentiality. Their actuality consists in their having existence at a given time, as well as the manner or nature of that existence. Their potentiality consists in all the ways that they could potentially exist (or cease to exist) in the future. An acorn, for example, has the actuality of a relatively small seed, but it has the potential to become a large tree. The argument from motion hinges on the notion that a potentiality possessed by something can only be activated or brought into existence by something that is already actually existing and has the power to activate the potentiality. No potentiality can activate itself, since it lacks the actual existence needed to function as a cause. Therefore, if change must be a matter of something potential becoming activated by what is already actual, every change must involve something that is changed and something distinct from what is changed that effects the change.

The next thing to consider is the assertion made by Gerhard that the sequence of potentialities being activated cannot go backwards forever. There cannot be, in other words, an infinite regress of changes. This is because if there were no first actuality that changed or put into motion everything else, there would be no explanation for how the sequence of things becoming actual ever got started. This is what Gerhard means when he says that secondary moving things do not move unless there is a first motion.

The argument from motion, therefore, shows that change requires that there be a first actuality or a first mover that is not itself actualized by anything else. As such, this first mover will have to exist eternally and independently (or without need of other things). Moreover, it must have the power to set everything else in motion, or account for all the changes present in creatures from the beginning of the universe until the end. Gerhard thus notes that this first actuality from which all other actuality proceeds must be identified with God, for only the name of God is suitable for such a reality.

3.5 What is the argument from efficient causation?

Another similar cosmological argument is the argument from efficient causation. An efficient cause is simply anything which by some exercise of power brings an effect into existence. This argument has essentially the same structure as the previous argument, but it focuses on the reality of causation instead of motion or change. Gerhard provides a concise version of it (once again evidently taken from Aquinas) when he writes:

> In these sensible things we find that there is an order of efficient causes. Yet we do not find in these causes, nor is it possible, that anything can be the efficient cause of its own self, because in this case it would be prior to itself, which is impossible. Therefore because in cases of this sort there is no progression to infinity (from the fact that secondary causes do not act except in the power of the first cause), it is necessary that there be some first efficient cause. Everyone calls this "God." (*ONGT*, 60)

In this argument our attention is called to the fact that the universe everywhere shows us chains or sequences of causes and effects. A thing is brought into existence by various causes, and it in turn contributes to the making of various effects. Gerhard points out that nothing can be its own cause, since then it would have to exist before itself. Therefore, everything that begins to exist or has the nature of an effect must be caused by something else that is before it in some sense. It is pointed out that any chain of causes cannot go on forever, because if there were no first cause, the chain itself would have no adequate explanation or ultimate source of its efficacy. This leads Gerhard to assert that there must be a first, uncaused cause that is the creator of all other causes. Such a cause is identified with God, because by nature such a cause could not begin to exist or be dependent on something else for its existence. Moreover, it would of necessity possess the power required to make it an adequate source of all other causes. As with the argument from motion, we are once again led by reasoning from efficient causality to the existence of an eternal, independent, and incredibly powerful being.

3.6 What is the argument from contingency?

Yet another cosmological argument is that from contingency. Although there is a form of an argument from contingency in Aquinas which is also used by Gerhard, I believe the best form of this argument is suggested by Leibniz. To understand how this argument works, we must first grasp the difference between contingent existence and necessary existence. A contingent being is one that, considered in itself, could either exist or not exist. Its non-existence is just as possible as its existence. A particular human being might exist, but he could just as well not exist. There is nothing about being human that makes it so that he must exist. As we all know, any given human being's existence depends on a variety of factors. By contrast, a necessary being is not the kind of being that could fail to exist. Its non-existence is impossible. It therefore must exist by its very nature.

If we look around us, we do not observe anything that has necessary existence. Everything we sense could possibly not exist. We know this, not only because there is evidence that the universe had a beginning, but also because everything changes, and any new state of existence will be caused by some previous state. What is caused or begins to be cannot have necessary existence. Therefore, the world around us is thoroughly contingent.

A question that a thoughtful person might ask is, why do all the things that could either exist or not exist in fact exist? In other words, looking at the big picture, why is there any universe of contingent beings at all? It appears that a contingent being must have a reason for its existence in something that has caused it to be. If that thing is itself contingent, then the cause will itself require a cause, and so on. Any chain of causes that is made up of contingent beings will thus have to be infinite unless it comes to an end in a necessary being. But once again, it must be noted that an infinite chain is not feasible, because then the chain itself would lack an explanation or reason for its existence. We are therefore required by reason to conclude that if there are contingent beings, there must be a necessary being. Since such a necessary being would have to exist as the being it is, it would have to be eternal, immutable (unchangeable), and independent, as well as the cause of all contingent beings. Moreover, it would have to be a spirit, since any physical being must be located in space and time and thus be able to undergo change in some way. It only makes sense, then, to call such a being God.

3.7 What are the most common objections to cosmological arguments?

We have now looked at three strong versions of the cosmological argument. It is important to note, however, the objections critics most often raise against these arguments and how you might answer them.

One objection is that there is no proof that everything that begins to exist has a cause or reason for its existence in some other being. As indicated earlier in this chapter, it appears to be correct that there is no proof, because there is not a more obvious proposition from which a person could infer that everything that begins to exist has a cause. But a lack of proof is irrelevant with respect to truths that possess this kind of self-evidence. For this is a principle that all sane people know intuitively and unconsciously assent to without fail when going about their daily lives. It is only denied in the context of discussing arguments for God's existence because people are looking for any means available to avoid assenting to the conclusion that God does in fact exist. Therefore, if presented with this objection, the best response is to ask the person if he is really being consistent. Is this a principle that he ever denies or doubts elsewhere? The person will have to grapple with how honest he is being with himself.

Another objection is that these arguments provide no proof that there exists a personal God that possesses intelligence and a will. This objection can be met by noting something important that obviously exists—namely, human beings. The ultimate cause of such beings must be adequate to produce them. But an impersonal reality could not be adequate to produce beings who are conscious, rational, and moral. It follows that the ultimate explanation of the universe must itself be conscious, rational, and moral.

Yet a third objection applies specifically to the argument from contingency. It alleges that if God is a necessary being, then his activity must be necessary, and therefore whatever he creates will not be contingent but necessary. This means that nothing could in fact be contingent, and therefore the argument from contingency would have nothing contingent from which to begin. In response, a few things need to be noted. We should recognize that something might be necessary in the sense that given the nature of its cause, it could not be otherwise, but this does not entail that it is necessary in itself or absolutely necessary. In fact, it could not possibly be necessary in itself, because as an effect, it would still be dependent on its cause, and nothing that is dependent in any way can be absolutely necessary. Therefore, asserting that a necessary being is the source of contingent beings is not absurd. Now it might be pointed out that this still leaves us with a deterministic universe (that is, one in which all events are predetermined), since all contingent effects would necessarily be produced by their causes if the activity of the first cause were necessary. In other words, there would be no "room" for indeterminism to appear or arise if the foundation of everything were absolutely necessary. In response, I think it has to be conceded that there is no obvious answer here, and that the indeterminism and freedom we witness in the universe is a mystery. But at this point, we are dealing with issues that are not immediately related to the matter of God's existence. The argument from contingency can still sufficiently demonstrate that a necessary being exists, even if we are not able to unravel every difficulty that seems to follow from this conclusion.

One last objection, which is based on a deep misunderstanding of the nature of God, is the objection that if everything needs a cause, then God must require a cause too. In response, we should point out that this necessity only arises in the case with things that begin to exist, because such things do not begin to exist without any reason. In the case of God, we are dealing with a reality that never began to exist and could not begin to exist, because he exists necessarily. This being the case, it makes no sense to ask the question what caused him to be.

3.8 What is a teleological argument?

Another kind of *a posteriori* argument is the category of teleological arguments, which are sometimes referred to as arguments from design. As already mentioned, with such arguments we are not starting from general features of the universe but from our observations of particular instances of order and purpose in the natural world. These arguments take a variety of forms, depending on what in particular is highlighted as an instance of order. Gerhard articulates the version of this argument found in Aquinas when he writes the following:

> We see not only beings endowed with reason but also those things that lack knowledge operating to achieve a definite goal, because always or quite frequently they work in the same way and achieve their goals through due means. From this it is clear that they are acting not fortuitously and by chance but that those operations are coming from the intent of some intelligence that directs them. This intelligence we call "God." (ONGT, 60–61)

Gerhard is claiming here that things without any intelligence or knowledge seem to commonly operate for specific purposes. But if, lacking intelligence, they cannot direct themselves to fulfill these purposes, then they must be directed by something else that intends that they realize them. The knowledge and power required to direct them in this manner could only be possessed by God. The basic point here is a simple one: The natural world is full of orderly operations and regular patterns, and such order requires an explanation. Many things in nature, since they lack intelligence, cannot order their own acts; they therefore must be ordered by another who is capable of doing so. Only God could conceivably meet this need.

3.9 How might someone object to a teleological argument?

Someone who is very bold might assert that order and regularity in nature do not need any explanation. But no thoughtful person will be satisfied with such a response. Contingent order must be adequately explained just like anything else that is contingent. If someone denies this need, then such a person cannot be reasoned with, at least with respect to the considerations raised by this argument.

A much more common objection to teleological arguments is that whatever order is in the world can be explained by purely natural causes. Patterns and regularities, it is often alleged, may emerge simply through the random workings of nature. One reason why Darwinian evolution has proven to be so attractive to a certain type of person is that it appears to provide just such a natural explanation of order. But Darwinism, even if true, would only suffice to explain a limited range of orderly phenomena. It has nothing to say about the order and regularity of all the non-living things that occupy the universe. Moreover, a logical difficulty remains even in the case of those living things that are allegedly explained by Darwinism.

This difficulty can be described in the following way. Order in anything that begins to exist cannot be entirely self-caused. This is because a thing is defined as the thing it is due to the order that it has, and there is no living thing that, at the beginning of its existence, is nothing in particular and then makes itself to be something. This means that the order it has when it first comes into existence needs to be received from its cause. However, its cause cannot give what it does not itself have; it must in some sense also possess order. If the cause also had a beginning, then it will need its initial order explained by something else, and so on. Ultimately, no living being that itself had a beginning will be able to be the original source of order for all living things that had a beginning, since it will need its own order explained.

It is evident, therefore, that we cannot look to living contingent things to account for their own order. And we have already seen that order in non-living contingent things clearly requires an explanation. We will not be able to find this explanation in unliving and unthinking matter, since something without intelligence could never be an adequate or sufficient explanation of order. We must therefore go beyond matter to affirm the reality of a source of order outside of the physical universe, one that is not itself derived from any prior source. This source could only be the intelligence, wisdom, and power of God.

It might be noted here that insofar as beauty requires order, beautiful things are also capable of providing a starting point for inferring God's reality.

3.10 What is a moral argument?

Moral arguments come in several forms. Perhaps the most straightforward proceeds from the existence of moral obligations. All people, even those who profess that morality is completely unreal or subjective, seem compelled to believe in their everyday lives that moral obligations exist. Most, when asked if people have an obligation to refrain from committing murder, are entirely certain that there is such an obligation and almost as sure that it could not be otherwise. The question is, granting the assumption that there are moral obligations which are objective and necessary, what explains their existence? It seems evident that no human being's opinion or preference could be the basis of their reality, since no human opinion has the character of necessity. Human opinions can always change. Moreover, it is not at all clear why one person's beliefs about moral obligations could ever make such obligations exist objectively or be obligatory for others. What is needed, then, is a ground of moral obligations in something that is necessary and authoritative—either a necessary will or necessary nature that is in a position to issue objectively binding commands. Furthermore, since moral obligations are not physical or material things, the source of their existence will clearly have to be something immaterial or spiritual. We are therefore justified in thinking that the reality of moral obligations can only be properly accounted for by the existence of a necessary, spiritual being who is in a position of authority with respect to all other beings. And this, of course, is most naturally thought of as God.

Another, somewhat different formulation of this type of argument is found in Gerhard. He writes:

> If there is some natural distinction of the just and the unjust in all men, surely there also exists in all men some natural knowledge of God. This is the reason: No one recognizes the distinction between right and wrong except by comparison with the divine Law, which is the norm and rule of all righteousness. If, then, there is a natural distinction between right and wrong in all humans, surely there is also in them the knowledge of divine Law. But where there is a knowledge of the divine Law, there is also some knowledge of God as the Lawgiver on the basis of related things and the necessary connection of cause and effect. He who knows the divine Law knows that God exists, because He is the only Lawgiver. . . . If the knowledge of the Law is natural to man, so is the knowledge of God. (*ONGT*, 72)

Gerhard is essentially saying here that true moral judgments must have reference to an objective, authoritative, and immutable moral law, whether this law is known by means of the human conscience or by what the Bible says. Such a law in turn must have a lawgiver or source—in other words, something that gives it the character of a law. No human being or other creature can be the source of this law, because no creature can account for its objectivity, immutability, and authoritativeness. God alone therefore must be its source.

3.11 What objections are there to moral arguments?

Perhaps the easiest way to attack a moral argument is to deny that moral obligations have any reality. If this were the case, then there would not be anything that requires an adequate explanation. A person might say that to assert that something should be done is simply to indicate that one likes it, and to say that something should be avoided is nothing more than to express one's displeasure concerning it. The best way to respond to such a claim is simply to ask the person making it to ask himself if he really believes that people have no obligation to abstain from heinous and horrific deeds. My own view is that no one really believes this, and their actions will prove it, though there are people who will dishonestly claim to believe it in order to avoid acknowledging the reality of God's existence.

Another objection is sometimes raised by claiming that the ground of our moral obligations could be impersonal. A skeptic thinking along these lines might suggest that the fact that murder is wrong is a necessary and authoritative truth in the same way that 2 + 2 = 4. But just as 2 + 2 = 4 does not obviously imply the existence of God, neither does the fact that murder is wrong. In response, it should first be noted that it is arguable that 2 + 2 = 4 does imply the existence of God, as we will see in a moment when we look at the argument from eternal truths. But let us grant for the sake of argument that it does not. There is still a problem for the critic in that obligation seems inseparable from the notion of accountability. When we say a person has an obligation to do something, we also intend to assert that he will be accountable for either doing or not doing it. In other words, he will justly be subject to either reward or punishment. If such a person were in no way accountable for an action, it is hard to see in what sense he could be said to have an obligation to do or avoid it. Accountability, however, clearly seems to require a personality to whom a person is accountable. One cannot be accountable to an inanimate object, or to an impersonal force. It follows that if objective obligations are inseparable from accountability, then the source of these obligations must be inseparable from a personality to whom people are accountable. Therefore, it only makes sense to hold that the ultimate ground of all obligation and accountability is one and the same being, and that this being must be personal.

3.12 What is the argument from eternal truths?

There is an interesting and quite strong argument for the existence of God that primarily comes from the insights of St. Augustine. The form in which I present it here is found in the *Handbook of Christian Apologetics*, by Peter J. Kreeft and Robert K. Tacelli. This argument asks us first to consider that human minds can know eternal and necessary truths, such as those of logic, mathematics, and morals. It then makes the claim that such truths can only exist in a mind. For example, the proposition that murder is wrong would not have any reality of any kind if there were no mind to conceive of it. However, it is clear that human minds are not eternal, since they all begin to exist at a particular time. Hence, if these truths are always and everywhere true, and could not be otherwise, then there must be an eternal, omnipresent mind that always knows them. Such a mind would of course have to be God's.

3.13 How might such an argument be criticized?

This argument may be objected to by either denying that there are eternal truths or that true propositions must exist in minds in order to exist at all, but it is difficult to see any good reasons to accept either claim. The former seems absurd, and regarding the latter, it can be said that a proposition is an entirely abstract object, and apart from the activity of minds, purely abstract objects have no evident reality.

3.14 What is the argument from desire?

The final argument that will be considered is the argument from desire. This argument is most commonly connected to C. S. Lewis, but it has its origins in many writers before Lewis's time, including St. Augustine. The argument asks us to consider as a starting point that all of our natural desires have means by which they can be satisfied. For example, our desire for food can be met by eating, and our desire for companionship can be met by other people. There is one natural desire that we all have, however, that can never be satisfied by anything we experience in this world. This is our desire for everlasting happiness. Since all of our other natural desires have objects that can satisfy them, it would be very strange if in this one instance we were to have a desire that nothing could satisfy. The argument concludes that since there is no good reason to posit an exception, we should grant that an object that can meet this desire most likely exists as well. Such an object would have to itself be eternal and possess all of the values needed to ensure our happiness. Hence it would have to be good, true, beautiful, and so forth. It would only make sense to identify such a being as God.

3.15 What objections might be offered to the argument from desire?

There are two objections that are most likely to be raised. One is the claim that an individual has no such desire for everlasting happiness. A person might claim to be perfectly satisfied with finite things and the prospect of a finite lifespan. The only response to this objection, as with some others, is to ask such a person if he is really being honest with himself. It seems highly unlikely, because most people are constantly indicating in various ways how unsatisfied they are with these things. The other objection is that this argument starts from a subjective characteristic of human beings and therefore cannot conclude to the reality of something objective. But the desire which serves as the starting point of the argument is not merely a subjective feeling but a general feature of human psychology. Therefore, it is as objective as human nature itself, and as real as the conclusion to which it leads.

This concludes our discussion of arguments for God's existence. Although others could be mentioned, in my opinion the preceding arguments are likely to be the most useful in the context of ordinary conversations with people. In the next chapter, we will turn to how you might begin to make a case for the truth of specifically Christian beliefs.

For Further Reading

Craig, William Lane. *The Cosmological Argument from Plato to Leibniz*. Eugene, OR: Wipf and Stock, 2001.

Davies, Brian. *Thinking about God*. Eugene, OR: Wipf and Stock, 2010.

Feser, Edward. *Five Proofs of the Existence of God*. San Francisco: Ignatius Press, 2017.

_____. *Scholastic Metaphysics: A Contemporary Introduction*. Heusenstamm, Germany: Editiones Scholasticae, 2014

Gerhard, Johann. *On the Nature of God and on the Trinity*. Ed. Benjamin T. G. Mayes, trans. Richard J. Dinda. St. Louis: Concordia, 2007.

Kreeft, Peter, and Ronald K. Tacelli. *Handbook of Christian Apologetics*. Downers Grove, IL: InterVarsity, 1994.

Levering, Matthew. *Proofs of God: Classical Arguments from Tertullian to Barth*. Grand Rapids, MI: Baker Academic, 2016.

Spitzer, Robert J. *New Proofs for the Existence of God: Contributions of Contemporary Physics and Philosophy*. Grand Rapids, MI: Eerdmans, 2010.

4

The Reliability of the New Testament

At this point, we have provided arguments to establish the truth of theism, or the view that God exists. In this chapter, we will begin to make a case for the truth of Christianity. Perhaps the simplest way to state why Christianity is evidently true is to call attention to the existence of the church. For it is impossible to see how the church could exist today if the claims that Christianity makes about its origins were not true. No alternative explanation can possibly suffice. In order to see why this is the case, we need to take a close look at the resurrection of Jesus, which will enable us to see that only the church's traditional view of this event can account for why the church exists at all. However, since our primary source of information about the resurrection is the New Testament, it will be helpful to first establish that the New Testament is generally reliable in what it tells us about the first-century events that it relates. It is to this concern, then, that we will turn in the present chapter.

4.1 How do we know the New Testament we have today is identical with the original writings?

This question concerns the transmission of the text of the New Testament books from the time they were written up to today. Since the advent of printing, we have no shortage of evidence that the New Testament has remained substantially the same. The millions of Bibles that have been printed over the past six hundred years make this clear. But what happened between the first century and the beginning of printing in the fifteenth? During this time, only handwritten manuscript copies of the New Testament existed. It is often asserted by skeptics with little knowledge of the facts that there was a great deal of alteration made to the text during this time. The people involved in copying Bibles, they imagine, were not opposed to changing the wording to bring it more in line with what they preferred to believe. The skeptics also commonly assume that even apart from intentional modifications, the accuracy of the text doubtless deteriorated over time due to errors in copying, much like how in a children's game of telephone the message at the end is often quite different than what it was at the beginning.

This way of imagining matters, however, is not congruent with the facts. First of all, it is not the case that as new copies were made, all the old copies disappeared, and thus were unavailable to confirm the correctness of the new copies. The rather staggering truth is that even though the original writings were not preserved, we do possess a huge number of manuscript copies of the New Testament made before the dawn of printing. Over five thousand copies in the original Greek have been preserved, and this does not even include the thousands of copies that exist in Latin, Coptic, Syriac, and other languages. While it must be conceded that we have many more manuscripts from the Middle Ages than from the earliest centuries of the church, it is nevertheless the case that we possess hundreds of ancient copies in various states of completeness. The oldest complete New Testament manuscript dates back to the first half of the fourth century, and there are many earlier ones that contain significant parts of it. We even have fragments of manuscripts that are from the first half of the second century, and therefore date to a time less than a hundred years from when the New Testament was written.

It should also be mentioned in this connection that we have many more manuscript copies of the New Testament than we do of other ancient texts, such as those composed by Homer, Plato, or Aristotle. Hence, if we are skeptical about our ability to know what the New Testament originally contained, we should be much more skeptical about these other writings. However, no one really is, which indicates that skepticism about the integrity of the New Testament documents is generally driven by bias against the Bible more than anything else.

In comparing these thousands of extant copies, scholars have found that there is a surprising amount of consistency between them; 99.5% of the time any two copies will agree. This agreement can be explained by a couple of important factors. One is that it is evident that copies were made very carefully. The people copying the Scriptures knew it was incredibly important that they not make mistakes, since this was the word of God. Another factor is that so many copies were made, and their texts quoted so often by early Christian teachers and writers, that it would have been obvious if any one copy significantly departed from the text of other manuscripts. Early Christians knew the Bible quite well, because significant portions of it were regularly read during their worship. The learned among them who were able to study the Bible themselves would no doubt have been able to identify any copy with substantial errors.

This is not to say or suggest that the copies we have are virtually free from minor discrepancies. There are discrepancies, which is only to be expected when one considers that we are talking about thousands of handmade copies of rather lengthy texts. But the emphasis must be placed on the word *minor*. The discrepancies generally in no way affect the meaning of the text. In the relatively few cases where they do, no significant doctrine is undermined thereby. Moreover, extensive comparison of manuscripts can usually indicate when a change in the text entered into a series or "family" of copies. This means that most such changes can be recognized, and the original form of a given text can be distinguished from the forms it took after errors were introduced.

Given all of these factors, most scholars today are confident that we are able to know with almost complete certainty what the original text of the New Testament was. There are a few dozen verses where the original wording is still not entirely certain to contemporary researchers, but no doctrine depends on our being able to identify with certainty the wording of these verses. We can have assurance, therefore, that the Bibles we have today do not deviate in any important way from the original texts of the New Testament books.

4.2 What reasons do we have to believe that what was originally written is true?

This naturally raises the issue, however, of whether or not the documents as they were originally written were truthful. Excellent copies of the original writings would be irrelevant if these writings were filled with errors or falsehoods by their authors. There are a few specific questions that must be answered in considering this matter. First, were the writers of the New Testament books in a position to know the truth of the things they wrote about? Second, did they have any obvious motive for being dishonest? Third, are there any signs in the New Testament itself that these writings are unreliable? Fourth, is there any corroborating evidence from other ancient sources that the New Testament authors were truthful? If we can provide affirmative answers to the first and fourth of these questions, and negative answers to the second and third, then we will have sufficiently established the reliability of the New Testament.

4.3 Were the New Testament writers in a position to know the truth about the things they wrote about?

Two of the main ways that skeptics attempt to cast doubt on the trustworthiness of the New Testament is by claiming that we do not know who the authors of many books were, and that the books were written long after the events they describe. If these claims were true, it would indeed give us little reason to be confident about the truthfulness of these writings. However, there are no good reasons to believe that either claim is well-founded. The early church placed its confidence in these books very early on precisely because it was sure that they were from reliable sources, and the church at this time was naturally in a better position to trace the pedigree of the manuscripts than modern critics.

The evidence we have from the earliest writings produced by Christians after the New Testament was completed is that all the New Testament books were written by people in a position to know what they were talking about. During the first and second centuries a criterion was employed to ensure that only reliable testimony about Jesus and his significance would be considered authoritative. This criterion was that a writing had to have been written by an apostle or someone who was a close acquaintance of an apostle. All the New Testament writings that were universally regarded as authoritative at this time were understood to meet this standard. According to these early Christian writers, the author of the Gospel of Matthew was indeed Jesus' disciple Matthew. The author of the Gospel of Mark was John Mark, a close associate of the apostle Peter. The Gospel of Luke and the Acts of the Apostles were composed by a companion of the apostle Paul, the physician Luke. And John was written by Jesus' beloved disciple, John. With the exception of the Letter to the Hebrews, there were no doubts that the letters attributed to Paul were in fact written by Paul.

We have no good reason to think that the early church was unaware of or badly confused about the truth of these matters. Moreover, the New Testament writings themselves have clues that suggest that their authors possessed a high level of familiarity with the events they wrote about. Details are provided that we would not expect to be noted by someone who did not know much about what originally happened. The fact that some important later events are not written about (such as the destruction of Jerusalem in A.D. 70 or the death of the apostle Paul) also lends credibility to the contention that these writings were written at a time close to the events they describe. It is only reasonable, then, to hold that the authors of the New Testament books were able to know the truth of the events they wrote about.

Sometimes skeptics attempt to cast doubt on the contents of the New Testament in another way, namely, by pointing out that we know of other ancient writings about Jesus that were allegedly written by apostles, writings which contradict in various ways those found in the New Testament. The claim is sometimes made that these texts are possibly more truthful, and that the early church might have suppressed the truth in denying these writings a place in the collection of books that make up the New Testament. In response, it must be pointed out that there is no factual basis for such a view. Virtually all modern scholars agree that nearly all of these writings were written after the books that make up the New Testament. Some of them were composed centuries later. The reason these books were not regarded as authoritative by the early church was that they lacked the provenance that the books which entered the canon possessed. In other words, there was insufficient evidence that these books had any genuine connection to the testimony of an apostle. The fact that such writings, moreover, often contradicted books that were known to have such a connection only sealed their fate. It would have been highly irresponsible for the early church to give these books any credence or lend them any legitimacy. Thankfully, their commitment to preserving the apostolic faith prevented them from doing so.

4.4 Did the authors of the New Testament have any motive for being dishonest?

The answer to this question is quite simply no, they did not. It is always of the utmost importance to remember the precarious and dangerous position occupied by Christians in the first century. Christians were often subject to extreme persecution, and being a Christian would never have been a path to higher social status. Even within Christian communities, there would have been very few worldly or material incentives to seek leadership positions or dishonestly maintain that the claims of Christianity were true. The apostle Paul gives us a striking portrait of what life was like for an early Christian leader, and there is nothing about it that suggests that such a life was a pathway to worldly success or comfort (2 Cor. 11:23–33). Consequently, lying about the events that the church was founded upon would make no sense. There would be no rewards for doing so here on earth, and a person could not expect that God would reward dishonesty in heaven. Hence, there is no reason to think that the New Testament writers had any motive for being dishonest.

4.5 Does the New Testament itself bear any signs that it cannot be trusted?

Once again, the answer to this question must be no. There are some differences in the various accounts of some events, but this is to be expected, as different witnesses would see and remember things from slightly different points of view. Such accounts can all be correct, insofar as they each point to different but real aspects of an event. Moreover, these slight differences provide grounds for concluding that the New Testament writers were not simply copying each other or working together to try to "get their story straight."

That being said, on the whole it should be acknowledged that there is a remarkable degree of consistency immediately evident when we read the

New Testament books. The accounts appear harmonious. The fact that there is such a high degree of consistency, but that not all accounts are exactly the same, indicates that we have several authors providing truthful accounts from their own points of view.

4.6 Is the truth of the New Testament corroborated by external evidence?

Though evidence outside the New Testament for the truth of what it relates is rather limited, there are some important pieces of data. In the realm of archaeology, numerous finds have supported the view that the New Testament is trustworthy. Various people and places mentioned in the New Testament, such as Pontius Pilate, Caiaphas, and the Pool of Bethesda have been shown to have really existed.

There is also corroborative evidence to be found in ancient texts written by non-Christian authors. It is important to keep in mind that we cannot expect such sources to affirm everything that the Christian sources do, otherwise the non-Christian authors would be indistinguishable from Christian authors. However, what they do confirm is valuable nonetheless. In the first century, the Jewish historian Josephus (37–ca. 100) made important references to Jesus, James the brother of Jesus, John the Baptist, and Herod the Great. The Roman historian Tacitus (ca. 56–ca. 120) also referred to Christ and stated that he was executed. Other pagan writers from near this time who mentioned Christ in their writings are the Roman governor Pliny the Younger (61–ca. 113), and Lucian (ca. 125–ca. 180).

It should now be sufficiently clear that the New Testament can be regarded as a collection of reliable documents. At this point, we have not yet made a case that they are infallible or without errors of any kind, but we have shown that there is no good reason to doubt their general veracity. We know what the original form of the text was, and we know that the authors of the New Testament books were in a position to write what was true. Furthermore, it is clear that they had no reason to be dishonest or to intentionally mislead. This being so, we can now advance to making the all-important case that

Jesus did in fact rise from the dead on Easter morning, as the church has always confessed.

For Further Reading

Barnett, Paul. *Is the New Testament Reliable?* 2nd ed. Downers Grove: IL: IVP Academic, 2004.

Bauckham, Richard. *Jesus and the Eyewitnesses: The Gospels as Eyewitness Testimony*. Grand Rapids, MI: Eerdmans, 2006.

Blomberg, Craig. *The Historical Reliability of the New Testament*. Nashville: B&H Academic, 2016.

Bruce, F. F. *The New Testament Documents: Are They Reliable?* 6th ed. Downer's Grove, IL: InterVarsity, 1981.

Keener, Craig S. *Christobiography: Memory, History, and the Reliability of the Gospels*. Grand Rapids, MI: Eerdmans, 2019.

Metzger, Bruce M. *The Canon of the New Testament: Its Origin, Development, and Significance*. Oxford: Oxford University Press, 1987.

_____. *The Text of the New Testament: Its Transmission, Corruption, and Restoration*. 3rd ed. Oxford: Oxford University Press, 1992.

5

The Resurrection of Jesus

The resurrection of Jesus is the foundation of the Christian faith. If it really happened, then Christianity is true. If it did not, then Christianity is false. It really is that simple. The apostle Paul acknowledged this when he wrote to the Corinthians that if Christ is not risen, then their faith is useless (1 Cor. 15:17). This being the case, it is of the highest importance that we establish beyond a reasonable doubt that the resurrection was a real event in history. Thankfully, this can be done, and without great difficulty. For the truth is that only the reality of the resurrection is consistent with what we know happened in the early years of the church. No other theory of what happened accords with all the relevant facts. In this chapter we will do three things. First, we will examine the reasons we have to believe that the resurrection occurred. Next, we will briefly examine the most common alternative theories of what happened after Jesus' death, and indicate why they are absurd or at least entirely inadequate. Lastly, we will examine some common objections to the possibility of miracles. These will be shown to be groundless.

5.1 What reasons can be given to support the reality of the resurrection?

There are several points that can be made in this connection. One is that it is evident that even Jewish opponents of the early Christians conceded that Jesus' tomb was empty and his body was missing. Another is the claim of multiple New Testament writers that Jesus was seen by many people after he died. If this were untrue, it is unlikely that multiple people highly familiar with the events of Jesus' life and death would all have agreed in saying that it happened. The assertion would also most likely have been disputed or corrected by Jesus' disciples if it were false. But there is no sign of any such thing having happened. A further piece of evidence is that Jesus' brothers seem to have been moved to believe in him only after his death (John 7:5, Gal. 1:19). It is nigh impossible to explain how they would have come to believe that a crucified man was the promised messiah if something remarkable had not transpired that changed everything. The apostle Paul claimed to have seen the resurrected Christ when that was the last thing on earth he expected or wanted to see. Certainly in his case there was no kind of wishful thinking involved.

The most powerful piece of evidence, however, comes from the actions of Jesus' disciples after his death. Not only did they all agree in claiming that he was risen and had been seen by many people (an agreement which is remarkable in itself), but they lived their lives as if this were true. Nothing is a clearer sign of what someone really believes than what that person does. And the actions of Jesus' disciples make it plain that they believed that he had been raised from the dead. All of them devoted their lives to spreading the good news about him. All of them suffered hardship, persecution, and in most cases death for their efforts. As mentioned in the previous chapter, there were no worldly incentives for being an apostle of Jesus Christ, so there was absolutely no motive for any kind of dishonesty or deception on their part. Given this behavior, we have to assume that they really believed that Jesus was raised. And given that there were several of them, and that they appear to have been people who were clearheaded and able to exercise good judgment (as we see in many places in the New Testament), we have to assume they were not deluded or mentally ill.

The foregoing considerations, brief as they are, are strong enough to warrant our full assent to the reality of the resurrection. There are, however, some popular alternative views of what happened, and it will be helpful to address them.

5.2 Is it possible that Jesus did not really die?

This view is sometimes called the swoon theory. The basic idea is that Jesus did not actually die on the cross; he merely passed out or appeared to be dead. After he was taken down and placed in the tomb, he somehow was able to revive, and his disciples later saw him after he had recovered and left the tomb. The defects in this theory are numerous. First, we can note that Roman soldiers knew how to do their job. They were expert executioners, and they would not mistake someone who had merely passed out for someone who was dead. The spear that pierced Jesus' side would have been driven into his heart and lungs by someone who knew what he was doing. This spear thrust was meant to make absolutely certain what was already quite evident. Second, even if Jesus were somehow still living when placed in his tomb, the amount of physical suffering inflicted on him would have made it extremely unlikely that he could have survived long without medical treatment. It is certainly implausible that he would have been able in such a condition to exit his tomb given the fact that it was secured by a large stone and guarded by soldiers. Third, the New Testament writers report that Jesus appeared to them with a glorified body, not a half-crucified and tortured body. Certainly the disciples would have been able to distinguish between a Jesus who was somehow able to barely survive his own crucifixion and a Jesus who had entered a new state of existence altogether. Fourth, if Jesus had not really died on the cross, then presumably Jesus would have remained on earth, and at some point he would have truly died. The ascension is no less miraculous than the resurrection, so to believe the former and doubt the latter makes no sense at all. His disciples in such a scenario would presumably have known that he was still living on earth and becoming older like everyone else. But there is no suggestion anywhere that anyone believed this. It is thus safe to say that the swoon theory has nothing to recommend it.

5.3 Is it possible that Jesus' disciples stole his body?

This was an assertion commonly made by unbelieving Jews in the early centuries of the church. These Jews acknowledged that Jesus' tomb was empty, but they refused to imagine that he could actually have risen from the dead. There are insurmountable difficulties with such a theory. First, the Romans had placed soldiers as guards at Jesus' tomb to prevent any such mischief. That these professional soldiers would be so derelict in their duty as to allow a ragtag group of Jesus' followers to remove his body and make off with it is unbelievable. It should be noted that the soldiers themselves would have been subject to death for such a failure to obey orders. Moreover, it is clear that after Jesus' arrest and death the disciples were extremely demoralized and fearful of the authorities. It makes no sense to think they saw something to gain from stealing his body and then agreeing to lie about it. Even more difficult for this theory to explain is how the disciples then devoted the remainder of their lives to boldly spreading this lie while being subject to intense persecution with no hope of worldly reward. Lastly, not one of Jesus' followers ever admitted that the story of the resurrection was the result of some kind of plot. All things considered, then, the stolen body theory is patently absurd.

5.4 Could it have happened that the disciples were merely hallucinating when they saw Jesus?

If the claim of the New Testament were that only one disciple saw Jesus after his death, or perhaps a few at different times, then it might be somewhat plausible to think that hallucinations were involved. However, it is clear that Jesus appeared to multiple people at the same time. Paul writes that once he appeared to over five hundred people at one time (1 Cor. 15:6). There is no possible way that so many people experienced hallucinations of the same thing in the same way at the same time. Furthermore, this theory does nothing to explain the empty tomb. If people merely had visions of Jesus, his tomb should have still been occupied by his body. But it was not, and even the unbelieving Jews of the time admitted this. This idea that the resurrection appearances were hallucinations therefore cannot be regarded as credible.

5.5 Is it possible that the story of Jesus' resurrection only developed some time after his death?

On this view, the claim that Jesus rose from the dead is basically equivalent to a legend or a tall tale. Although commonly encountered, this theory is perhaps the least plausible of all, because it is opposed by the facts at every turn. The message of Jesus' resurrection was being widely spread within weeks if not days after his death. Simply put, there was no time for any legend to develop. The disciples did not go back to their regular lives and then years later, after a legend had arisen that Jesus rose—which they knew to have no basis in the facts—decide as a group to leave their jobs and homes to take on the difficult task of missionary work and eventual martyrdom.

Sometimes it is suggested, especially by proponents of liberal forms of Christianity, that the disciples knew that Jesus had remained dead, but they came to believe that his teachings were so valuable that these ought not die with him. They therefore began their ministry of sharing what Jesus had taught them and invented the resurrection as a symbol for the lasting importance of his message. There is nothing in the New Testament, however, that supports this idea. Moreover, and most importantly, the central theme of early Christian preaching was not Jesus' morals or his lifestyle but the very fact that he died for sinners and rose from the dead. If the resurrection were held to be just a symbol for how his way of life or moral teachings were of enduring importance, then early Christian preaching got things entirely backward. Hence, however it is construed, this theory is extremely implausible.

Since there are no really credible alternative theories, skeptics will sometimes simply retreat to the claim that miracles are unbelievable, so the resurrection cannot be admitted as true in any case. The contention here is that it really does not matter that there are no plausible natural explanations of the resurrection, because miracles are not things that any reasonable person can believe in anyway. Hence, whatever the real explanation is, it simply cannot involve a miracle. Given how common this line of thought is, it must be examined.

5.6 What is the objection to miracles?

A miracle can be defined simply as an event without any natural explanation. Some people contend that miracles are impossible because they are violations of the laws of nature. Since these laws are held to determine everything that happens in the universe, nothing that seems to break these laws can be admitted. However, this is an extremely weak claim. So-called laws of nature describe how things as a matter of fact generally go; there is no reason to think they describe how things must necessarily go. There is no scientific proof that the laws of nature somehow stipulate what is possible, nor in principle could there be. As long as we can point to a possible supernatural cause of an event with no natural explanation, there is nothing inconceivable about it. As we have already discussed several reasons to believe that God exists—a being who could doubtless cause a miraculous event to occur whenever and wherever he wanted—there is no reason a person should be absolutely opposed to the possibility of miracles.

A greater difficulty is presented by the claim that even though a miracle is possible, the unlikelihood of one occurring is so great that a person could not ever be justified in believing that one had actually happened. This is especially true given that deception, ignorance, and misunderstanding are relatively commonplace and thus function as superior explanations. This position was perhaps most famously set forth by the skeptical philosopher David Hume (1711–1776) during the Enlightenment. His argument, however, fails to undermine the case for the resurrection. For one thing, there are plenty of events in history considered to be well-established facts that were highly improbable or even unique. For example, a woman named Vesna Vulović survived a fall of over 10,000 meters without a parachute when the plane she was on crashed in 1972. If the mere unlikelihood of something occurring were to be the decisive factor in determining whether or not a person could be justified in believing it, then no one would be justified in believing any such events. However, every reasonable person does. Hence it is clear that the quality of the evidence that something occurred ought to be the decisive factor.

Another thing that a focus on mere improbability misses is the importance of the context of miracles. It is true that a random, seemingly pointless miracle would have an exceedingly low probability, and therefore we would be right to be doubtful that any alleged miracle fitting this description actually occurred. In such a case, we likely would need evidence even more extraordinary than the miraculous event itself to justify belief in it. However, a miracle that would decisively serve to further God's plans, or fulfill his promises, would actually have a high likelihood of occurring. Hence, if there is reason to believe that a miraculous event fits this description—and the resurrection certainly does—then there is no reason that belief in the miracle would be unjustifiable merely on the basis of improbability. For given God's revealed purposes, what is improbable is that the resurrection did not occur.

Lastly, we have already seen that in the case of the resurrection, there was no motive for deception, and no realistic possibility that the disciples misunderstood what had happened. The New Testament makes it clear that the interactions the disciples had with their risen Lord were with a person who was able to speak, eat, and be touched. Furthermore, his tomb was empty. There is thus no possibility that the disciples merely lacked some knowledge of the events surrounding Jesus' appearances that would have made it clear to them that the resurrection did not happen and that the appearances could not be trusted.

We have thus seen that there is simply no good alternative or objection to the traditional Christian claim that Jesus did in fact rise from the dead. Only the resurrection makes sense. This being so, we should be unhesitant in affirming that it in fact happened as described in the New Testament. We also should pay attention to how this event supports other Christian beliefs, such as the deity of Christ. Explicating how it does this will be our next concern.

5.7 If the resurrection really happened, what does this entail for other Christian beliefs?

Granting the truth of the resurrection, we immediately find ourselves faced with several important implications. First and foremost, it only makes sense to consider the resurrection as God's stamp of approval on Jesus' person and teaching. If Jesus had not been the promised messiah, if his character had been flawed and his teachings marked by errors, it is inconceivable that God would have raised him from the dead. For in doing so, God would have lent legitimacy to these flaws and errors. Since God did raise him from the dead, it follows that he was the promised messiah, that his character was without flaw, and that his teaching was error free.

We are thus justified in believing that everything Jesus taught is true. And since his teaching confirms or is the source of most fundamental Christian doctrines, this means that these doctrines must be true. Of first importance is in this connection is the matter of Christ's deity. In spite of what some skeptics think, the Gospels make it abundantly clear that Jesus believed and taught that he was God incarnate. It is true that he did not travel around Palestine simply telling people that he was God. But the claim was nonetheless made by him in more subtle ways. We see an example of this in his several "I am" sayings from the Gospel of John (John 6:35, 8:12, 8:58, 10:9, 10:11, 11:25, 14:6, 15:1). These indicate that Jesus was identifying himself with the God who had revealed himself to Moses in the burning bush. It is also evident in his claims to be one with the Father. His Jewish contemporaries understood this to be his meaning, for they accused him of blasphemy and even sought to stone him (John 8:58–59, 10:30–33). Jesus also did not deny it when others called him the Son of God or even God (Matt. 16:16–20, 26:63–64, John 1:49, 11:27, 20:28–29). If these things were untrue, any honest man would have denied them. But Jesus did not. In fact, he responded affirmatively. Likewise, people sometimes worshipped him, and Jesus accepted their worship without rebuking them for idolatry (Matt. 8:2, 14:33, John 9:38). Any honest Jew of Jesus' day who knew himself to be only a man would never have allowed this. A final thing that can be mentioned is that Jesus forgave sins, something that no mere man was authorized to do in Judaism (Matt. 9:2, Luke 7:48). If we regard all of these things in light of Jesus' vindication by his resurrection, we can be confident that he correctly understood himself to be divine.

Another aspect of his teaching that Jesus' resurrection proves to be true is his view of the Bible. It is certain that Jesus taught that the Old Testament is God's inspired word and therefore entirely true. All of his statements about the Old Testament unequivocally support this view. He not only taught that the doctrines or moral truths of the Old Testament were correct, but that the very words of these books must be regarded as infallible (Matt. 5:18, John 10:35). We can thus be confident on this basis that the Old Testament is without error. With regard to the New Testament, Jesus claimed that the Holy Spirit would lead the church into all truth (John 16:13). He also stated that the Spirit will speak through the apostles (Matt. 10:20). There can be little doubt that these words apply to the writings of the apostles and their companions that were recognized to be authoritative and therefore canonical by the early church. The New Testament, therefore, can also be justifiably regarded as without error.

With the Bible shown to be inerrant, the positive case for Christianity is essentially complete. If the Bible is without error, then Christianity and all of the doctrines clearly taught in Scripture are true. This is a conclusion that any Christian can only celebrate. This does not mean, however, that no other considerations are valuable or can serve to further confirm the truth of the Scriptures. One of these that should be briefly discussed is the significance of fulfilled prophecies in the Bible.

5.8 What is the significance of fulfilled prophecies for defending the truth of Christianity?

One of the oldest and most time-honored ways of establishing the truth of Christianity is to point to the reality of prophecies found in the Bible that have apparently been fulfilled. In particular, Old Testament prophecies that predicted the coming of the messiah and which were fulfilled by the life, death, and resurrection of Jesus have been appealed to since the dawn of the church as clear proofs that Jesus was the promised Savior of Israel. There are over a hundred such prophecies in the Old Testament, and some of them are startling in their clarity. No one who is familiar with the events of Christ's life, for example, can read the verses predicting a suffering servant in the book of Isaiah without seeing an amazing correspondence (Isa. 52:13–53:12).

These fulfilled prophecies are often discounted by Jews and unbelievers, however, who claim that they were not referring to the coming of Jesus and therefore could not have been fulfilled by him. Sometimes the assertion is made that the writers of the Gospels shaped their narratives to make it look like Jesus fulfilled prophecies, but that this was simply clever and agenda-driven storytelling. What should we make of these claims?

First, it must be admitted that what the prophets consciously intended when they wrote and what God intended in inspiring their words may not have always been strictly the same. No doubt the prophets' own understanding of their predictions was sometimes vague or marked by obscurity. That said, the sheer number of Old Testament prophecies that appear to have some clear relation to Jesus makes it quite difficult to regard as plausible any suggestion that there is no genuine connection. We have already seen that the writers of the Gospels had no motive to be dishonest, so there is no good reason to believe they were changing or misconstruing the facts to make it look like prophecies had been fulfilled. The Jesus they intended to portray was not a character formed by someone's imagination, but a historical figure. This means that if an Old Testament prophecy appears to predict an event that the Gospels tell us was fulfilled by Jesus, there is no good reason to think this did not happen. And when we consider the total number of prophecies that appear to have been fulfilled, it is clear that there is more at work here than mere coincidences. Hence, a total dismissal of evidence from fulfilled prophecy would be highly unreasonable. Fulfilled prophecy might not be the best foundation for a case for Christianity—that would arguably be the evidence for the resurrection—but it certainly lends strong support to its credibility.

As you can see from all that has been discussed up to this point, belief in the saving truths of Christianity is entirely reasonable. That being said, there are other issues that skeptics often raise or point to that need to be addressed, since they often undermine confidence in the results that we have so far established. Many people acknowledge that the positive case for Christianity appears quite strong, but they appeal to these other matters in an attempt to justify their decision to continue in a state of unbelief. It is therefore to these issues that we will turn in the next chapter.

For Further Reading

Bass, Justin W. *The Bedrock of Christianity: The Unalterable Facts of Jesus' Death and Resurrection*. Bellingham, WA: Lexham Press, 2020.

Beale, G. K., and D. A. Carson, eds. *Commentary on the New Testament Use of the Old Testament*. Grand Rapids, MI: Baker Academic, 2007.

Beck, W. David, and Michael R. Licona, eds. *Raised on the Third Day: Defending the Historicity of the Resurrection of Jesus*. Bellingham, WA: Lexham Press, 2020.

Bombaro, John J., and Adam S. Francisco, eds. *The Resurrection Fact:*

Responding to Modern Critics. Irvine, CA: NRP Books, 2017.

Geivett, R. Douglas, and Gary R. Habermas, eds. *In Defense of Miracles: A Comprehensive Case for God's Action in History*. Downers Grove, IL: IVP Academic, 1997.

Habermas, Gary R., and Michael R. Licona. *The Case for the Resurrection of Jesus*. Grand Rapids, MI: Kregel, 2004.

Pagán, Joshua A., *Paul and the Resurrection: Testing the Apostolic Testimony*. Irvine, CA: 1517 Publishing, 2020.

Rydelnik, Edwin, and Edwin Blum. *The Moody Handbook of Messianic Prophecy*. Chicago, IL: Moody, 2019.

Wenham, John. *Christ and the Bible*. 3rd ed. Eugene, OR: Wipf and Stock, 2009.

Wright, N. T. *The Resurrection of the Son of God*. Minneapolis: Fortress Press, 2003.

6

Is the Bible Marred by Contradictions?

One of the most common objections to the inerrancy of the Bible, an objection which often is considered adequate grounds for rejecting the truth of Christianity, is that the Bible is marked by contradictions. These come in two varieties. One consists of alleged contradictions within the text, where parts of Scripture are said to disagree with other parts of Scripture. The other consists of external contradictions, where it is held that the Bible disagrees with what we know to be true about other things. Both of these types are quite serious, for if it could actually be proven that such contradictions exist, it would deliver a severe blow to the positive case for Christianity that we have already made. Perhaps the blow would not be sufficient to knock our case down completely, but it might be enough to leave it shaken and our faith uncertain. It is therefore necessary that such claims be adequately addressed.

6.1 Do some verses of the Bible contradict other verses?

The Bible has obviously been in existence for centuries, and during that entire time certain difficulties have been known to be present in it. Christians did not need skeptics to point them out, for they were the first to identify them. By the word difficulty, I simply mean a place in the text where the correct interpretation becomes uncertain. Christians have always been well aware that these tensions existed, and that some of them were due to the fact that there were places where Scripture had the appearance of contradicting Scripture. It is important to note that throughout most of the history of the church, these difficulties were never seen as grounds for denying the truthfulness of the text. That claim was not made until the rise of modern biblical criticism during the Enlightenment. Earlier biblical interpreters had the humility to recognize that they were quite limited in their understanding and that simply because something in the Bible escaped their grasp did not mean that it was untrue or nonsense.

It might be asked, however, why God would permit the text to be marked by difficulties of any kind. Wouldn't it be preferable if the Bible were always free from obscurity and stated everything as plainly and simply as possible? The answer is, not necessarily. If the Bible were such a plain and simple book, we might cease to think we had something more to learn from it. We might come to feel that it is a boring or tiresome volume. We might become disappointed by how cut and dry it is, like instructions for how to assemble a piece of furniture. We might question whether its origins were truly divine. We should not therefore assume that God should have given us a different Bible than the one we have. The proper attitude to this matter is humility and a glad acceptance of what he actually has chosen to give us, which is an incredibly inspiring book of awesome beauty and inexhaustible depth.

We are still faced, however, with the question of whether or not there are contradictions in the Bible. The traditional approach of the church to this issue, and the only correct one if we are to approach the text in the right spirit, is to seek for a way of bringing the apparently contradictory texts into harmony. In most cases of alleged contradictions, this can be done, and often quite easily. This does not necessarily mean that any given harmonization will be the correct solution to an alleged contradiction, but having a harmonization available does remove the obstacle that the contradiction presents to the Bible's trustworthiness. For a detailed analysis of many such contradictions, I recommend consulting William Arndt's helpful book *Bible Difficulties and Seeming Contradictions*.

Here are a few examples of alleged contradictions and what, in my view, are their correct resolutions:

Alleged contradiction: In all of the Gospels except John, the cleansing of the Temple occurs at the end of Jesus' ministry, but in John it occurs at the beginning.

Solution: There is no impossibility that this happened twice. It may have occurred twice but only been mentioned once by each Gospel writer because that was considered sufficient.

Alleged contradiction: According to the Gospel of Matthew, Judas died by hanging, but according to the Book of Acts, he fell on the ground and burst open.

Solution: Maybe Judas's noose broke and he then fell.

Alleged contradiction: According to the Gospels of Matthew and Mark, there was one angel seen at the Jesus' tomb after his resurrection, whereas according to the Gospels of Luke and John, there were two angels present.

Solution: Perhaps one witness saw only one, but another witness observed two.

Several more such examples and their solutions could be given. Of course, it may be the case that we find ourselves unable to find a fully satisfactory harmonization. In such situations we either are unable to think of any way of resolving the apparent inconsistency, or any suggested harmonization seems highly implausible to us. Does that mean it might be time to admit that the Bible has a real contradiction in it? It would be presumptuous, given what we know about what Jesus believed about the Bible, to grant that it is. The prudent approach here is to admit that our comprehension, especially when it comes to the things of God, does not necessarily define the limits of truth. It is always possible that there is some resolution to the supposed contradiction that we have failed to notice or that we cannot know about given our limitations.

Maintaining this attitude should not be difficult for those who are willing to evaluate the Bible based on its overall consistency. For few alleged contradictions in the Scriptures are truly difficult to harmonize, and it is actually remarkable that a text written by so many different human authors at different times is as unified and coherent as it is. Given this impressive cohesiveness, we should be willing to give the Bible the benefit of the doubt regarding those few instances in which a plausible harmonization eludes us.

6.2 Is the biblical narrative contradicted by archaeology?

Another claim that is often made is that the Bible, particularly the Old Testament, is contradicted by archaeology. For example, it is claimed that there is no archaeological proof that the Exodus of the Hebrews from Egypt ever happened. The truth, however, is that in every case like this one there is no evidence that actually contradicts what the Bible says; there is simply a lack of conclusive evidence to confirm the Bible, and someone believes such evidence should have been discovered. But a failure to find evidence can never furnish a disproof of anything—only positive evidence can do that. And on the whole, it must be said that time and time again, archaeological discoveries have demonstrated that people, places, and events mentioned in the Bible really did exist or happen. There is not a single case of the Bible being shown to be untrue by an archaeological discovery. While it may be true that some things have surprisingly not been confirmed by discoveries, a discovery may still be forthcoming, or there may be some explanation unknown to us for why the evidence is missing. This being so, there is no case to be made that archaeology contradicts the Bible.

6.3 Is the creation story in the Bible contradicted by science?

Of all the ways in which the Bible is alleged to contradict supposed facts, this is probably the one that creates the most doubt and consternation. It is held by many that the Bible and modern science are irreconcilably opposed on the matter of creation, and some think that if science with its outstanding credentials and centuries-long track record of success teaches something that contradicts the Bible, so much the worse for the Bible. Even people who do not share this attitude have had their faith tested by the obvious divergence between what science is typically held to claim and what the Bible says.

There are a few things that are important to keep in mind when approaching this issue. One is that truth never contradicts truth. God's revelation in nature can never contradict his revelation in Scripture, because God cannot contradict himself. Whatever the facts of nature really indicate about the origins of the universe and life on earth must be accepted by any Christian as true. Another thing that must be remembered, however, is that human beings are fallible, and even a consensus of human opinion can be wrong. In the course of history, many things have been held to be true by virtually everyone in a given culture or society that no one believes today. A third thing worth noting is that the methods of science may be more useful or applicable in some cases or areas of inquiry than in others. It is not the case therefore that one must be either pro-science or anti-science. We can wonder if some claims made by scientists are correct without in any way denigrating science as a whole or being skeptical about all scientific research.

Now what are we to make of the obvious divergence between the biblical view of creation and that of modern science? Not a few people are happy to assert that there is no real problem because the Bible and science are talking about creation in two entirely different ways. On the one hand, the Bible is only telling us in a poetic fashion that God created the world, but it is not seeking to inform us of how God created the world. Science, on the other hand, is simply telling us how the universe developed; it is not seeking to tell us where everything came from or for what purpose it exists. This picture of the relationship between science and the Bible no doubt holds a certain appeal, which explains its popularity, particularly with Christians in mainline or liberal churches. But it fails to deal adequately with the deep differences between the Bible's supernatural and teleological understanding of creation and modern science's purposeless, materialist picture of the world's evolution. These differences cannot be glossed over simply by claiming that the Bible and science are talking about different things or answering different questions.

Perhaps the most glaring problem for the theory that the Bible and science are dealing with two different things is the matter of the fall. The Bible claims that the fall was a fact in history, and that it had serious consequences for the entirety of creation. Moreover, the entire storyline of the Bible, and key

Christian doctrines, depend on the fall being such a historical event. Some theologians in modern times have attempted to treat the fall as a myth or symbol for the human condition, but as a result, they have been forced to give virtually every other doctrine a different meaning than that which it possesses in the Bible. If the fall really happened as the Bible says it did, then the picture of the world's development provided to us by modern science simply cannot be correct in many respects. It seems we are then forced to choose: either the Bible is correct, or the consensus of modern science is correct; there is no way to persist in claiming that they are really talking about different things.

How can we address this problem in a way that will enable us to preserve our integrity as Christians who claim to love and seek the truth? It is my view that if we can show that Darwinian evolution is almost certainly false, then this will entail that the biblical account of the fall, and its attendant picture of creation, can be given the benefit of the doubt, since it is vouched for by Jesus' confidence in the Old Testament, and since no other plausible options are available. The key question, then, is why should we doubt the truth of Darwinian evolution?

There are more than a few people today who assert that anyone who doubts Darwinism is equivalent to someone who believes the Earth is flat. But this is simply a tactic to shut down debate, for the confidence of those who assert such things is not at all justified by the facts. As things stand now at the beginning of the twenty-first century, Darwinism is a theory in trouble. The fundamental problem is that as we have come to learn more and more about the complexity of living things, the mechanisms that Darwinism proposes to explain how life evolves have become less and less adequate. It is clear at this point that the Darwinian explanation of the existence of different species is improbable to the point of being a statistical impossibility. This is of course not readily admitted by those who are invested in maintaining the hold that Darwinism has on the popular imagination, such as avowed atheists and evolutionary biologists. For such people, Darwinism is an essential part of their worldview. However, they either are ignorant of the facts or are in what amounts to a state of denial. Without going too deeply into why

Darwinism is so improbable, a few important facts can be mentioned. The points made here are especially indebted to the writings of Stephen C. Meyer, so I encourage anyone to read his books if more details are wanted.

First, granting merely for the sake of argument that evolutionary biologists and paleontologists are correct about the age of fossil specimens, the fossil record does not support the claims of Darwinian evolution. Darwinism insists that evolution is a gradual process. But in the fossil record, new species often appear with little or no apparent precedent. The defender of Darwin might claim that a person cannot conclude that Darwinism is false simply because fossils of these predecessors have never been found. This is a fair point, but it definitely casts doubt upon Darwinism, especially since so many fossils from all over the world have been brought to light in the last century or two.

This absence of fossils is thus a significant problem, but it is not the primary reason why this theory should be rejected. That comes from the biology that studies the genetic information contained in cells. Darwin's theory in its contemporary form is based on the idea that there are occasional mutations in this genetic information that lead to organisms having different characteristics than their predecessors. Over time, as the number of useful mutations adds up, a new species emerges. The problem with this view is that we now know the complexity of this genetic information, and what the probability is of a beneficial random mutation actually occurring. Furthermore, we can calculate how probable the entire process would be that would take us by means of random mutations from a single-celled bacterium to a human being. The improbability of the first development is high enough to already be statistically impossible; the improbability of the second is so astronomical that it is mind-boggling.

Darwinists are generally willing to concede that a useful mutation is highly unlikely, but they point to the fact that we are dealing with countless organisms over unimaginably long stretches of time. Surely, they say, that can significantly improve the odds. Unfortunately for them, the odds are so bad to begin with that this really does not make any practical difference. The likelihood of one useful genetic mutation occurring at random is about 1 in

10^{77} or 1 in 10000000 0000000000 0000000000 0000000000 0000000000 0000000000 0000000000 0000000000. A responsible estimate is that the chances of one useful mutation randomly occurring given the amount of time and the number of organisms that Darwinians imagine have existed in the Earth's past is 1 in 10^{37}, or 1 in 10000000 0000000000 0000000000 0000000000. As can be seen, the odds do improve, but it is all in vain because the improbability remains so great. One useful mutation is nigh impossible, and we don't need just one useful mutation, but millions of them, to account for how species arose naturalistically. Random mutations will thus never suffice as an explanation of the existence of different species. We therefore find nothing in Darwinism that comes close to providing a plausible account of how single-celled organisms evolved into all of the forms of life that populate the earth today. And it should be noted that we have not even bothered to address the likelihood of a living cell capable of reproduction coming to exist by chance in the first place. Simply put, there is no chance at all, and every effort of scientists to create life in a laboratory has been an utter failure.

Darwinian evolution in its pure form therefore has nothing to recommend it to a thinking person. It might be argued by some, however, that although evolution without God appears impossible, there is no reason to think that God did not guide an evolutionary process rather similar to what Darwin envisioned. This theory, often called theistic evolution, tries to find a happy medium between creation and evolution in the interest of honoring both God and science. However, given the amount of supernatural intervention this would require at every step, such a guided evolutionary process would be no less miraculous than the idea that God specially created each species at a particular time. Every beneficial genetic mutation would itself have to be a miracle! Since the view that God specially created the various species is not only in line with what the Bible teaches but is a much simpler account of what happened, it is doubtless to be preferred.

To sum things up, given the statistical impossibility of Darwinism being a true explanation of the existence of human beings (or any other species), and the confidence of Jesus that the Old Testament is entirely true, it is completely justifiable to affirm the biblical belief that man was specially created by God and that the state of the universe as we experience it now is the result of the fall.

6.4 Is not the story of the flood contradicted by the facts?

This is another significant place where there is often thought to be some incongruity between the text of Scripture and extrabiblical evidence. Sometimes the claim is made that it is unrealistic to think that all of the world's animal species could have been placed on the ark. Others question where all the water came from or where it went. Still others claim that there is no geological evidence of a worldwide flood. In the interest of meeting such objections, some liberal Christians have claimed that a great flood might have occurred that was not quite as extensive as the Bible says. This, however, is not an option open to those who believe the Bible is inerrant and trustworthy in all that it asserts. What then should we say?

Virtually all objections to the flood account in Genesis seem predicated on believing that the flood was for the most part a natural event, and as such should be understood in naturalistic terms. Presupposing this understanding, it is held that the relevant information we have does not seem to add up. However, there is no reason that a Christian should see things from this point of view. The flood event could have been marked by any number of miraculous happenings and interventions. That being the case, there is no reason to assume it did not happen as the Bible describes.

6.5 Did not Jesus teach that history was going to come to an end in the lifetimes of at least some of his disciples? If so, wasn't this expectation obviously contradicted by subsequent events?

It has been a common view since at least the turn of the twentieth century to hold that Jesus prophesied that the world would end within a few decades and that it did not, which proves that he was mistaken. One of the verses most commonly appealed to in this connection is Mark 9:1 and its parallels in Matthew and Luke. Jesus says, "Assuredly, I say to you that there are some standing here who will not taste death till they see the kingdom of God present with power" (NKJV). How can we address the problem raised by this text?

It appears to be true that Jesus did encourage his disciples to look forward to the end of history. But when we say this, we must keep in mind that what Jesus intended to do was not to predict when history would end (he avoided doing this), but to remind his listeners that it was crucial that they not put off repentance or live as if they had a long future ahead of them. The time is always short for beings such as we are. Jesus, in speaking about the coming judgment, wanted to remind his disciples of this fact. Regarding the verse just now mentioned, although a person could interpret it to mean that Jesus made a mistake, there is nothing that forces anyone to reach such a conclusion. The kingdom of God coming with power could conceivably refer to Jesus' transfiguration, his resurrection, or his second coming. If there are good grounds for believing Scripture to be inerrant, then obviously we will not wish to interpret the passage as referring to the last of these options.

6.6 Does not Jesus dying in the place of others contradict what we know to be fair about punishment?

Some people cannot fathom how one person could take a punishment for others. Isn't that punishing the innocent and letting the guilty go free? How could that be right? The reason this difficulty arises in their minds is that they are not thinking of the union Christ has with believers. There is a sense in which Jesus dies for us, but there is also a sense in which our union with Jesus and identity with him as members of his body means that Jesus is simply taking on the burdens of his own family, team, or people. As we all know, when people are on a team together, the actions of one member, whether good or bad, can justly affect everyone else. No one thinks this is unfair. But this is basically the situation that exists between believers and Jesus; he is the captain of our team, and although what we do hurts him, what he does helps us.

Luther, following Scripture, compared this union of Christ with the members of his body to the union between a husband and wife. In a marriage, the husband and wife are legally joined so that what belongs to one is the rightful possession of the other. Thankfully, for us, there is likewise a "joyous exchange" between Christ and ourselves which is made real through faith. In this exchange, he takes upon himself all of our sins and the penalty for them, and we receive from him his perfect righteousness and the everlasting rewards it has earned.

A related issue sometimes raised is how the death of one man could suffice to erase the penalty for the world's sins. It is true that this would never be the case if Christ were a mere man, which is why theologies that strip Christ of his divinity end up stripping us of his righteousness as well. Any theology that does this destroys any basis for Christian hope. But Christ was both fully human and fully divine, and these natures were perfectly united in his person when he went to the cross. Because of this unity of natures, the death of his human body had infinite value due to the infinite value of the divine nature united to it.

6.7 Is the morality of the Bible contradicted by what people now know is right and wrong?

There is an assumption made by many people today that we somehow have better moral knowledge now than people possessed in the past. Many developments, such as increased rights for women and racial minorities, have led to the widespread acceptance of this notion. However, it is not the case that we actually have discovered any new moral principles. Every legitimate appeal for granting rights to minorities has been firmly based on truths that human beings have been aware of for millennia. At most, all that has happened as a result of these appeals is that we have grown more consistent in applying them. Therefore, it is not the case that there has been progress in moral knowledge.

Nonetheless, people sometimes claim that many of the moral principles that guided the actions of people in the past were wrong and need to be disregarded and replaced with new ideas about what is right and acceptable. Yet it is hard to see how they could know this. What they often seem to believe is that morality in the past was based on principles that often conflicted with human desires and inclinations, and that this was bad because it meant that sometimes people were unable to pursue their desires and were left unhappy as a result. Underlying this view appear to be a few assumptions: that human happiness is more important than anything else; that individuals are always the best judge of what makes for their happiness; and that people should be encouraged to do whatever makes them happy as long as other people are not obviously physically or emotionally harmed by it. But are any of these assumptions true?

The answer is no. At least, there is no necessity that anyone grant that they are true, and if Christianity is true, then they are all necessarily false. Regarding the first assumption, the Christian view is that God is more important than anything else, and human beings are only truly happy when they make him the center of their lives. Concerning the second assumption, fallen humans are actually the last people we should expect to give an accurate assessment of what will make them happy. Human history is full of stories of people seeking happiness in things that could not ultimately provide it. The last assumption is entirely false: We are not called to do what makes us happy, but to do what is good and what we were made to do. It is only when we do what we were created to do, namely, to love and worship God, that we find genuine and lasting happiness. Since we have good reasons to believe that Christianity is true, we also have good grounds to reject the view that a morality based on individual desires is right and represents a higher form of morality than that found in the Bible. The truth is that making the subjective desires of the human individual the beginning and end of all moral considerations indicates a terrible decline in moral insight.

Having addressed some of the most common ways in which the Bible is said to be contradictory, in the next chapter we will tackle arguably the most influential objection to theism and therefore to Christianity—the problem of evil.

For Further Reading

Arndt, William. *Bible Difficulties and Seeming Contradictions.* St. Louis: Concordia, 1987.

Geisler, Norman L., and Thomas Howe. *The Big Book of Bible Difficulties: Clear and Concise Answers from Genesis to Revelation.* Grand Rapids, MI: Baker, 2008.

Heimbach, Daniel R., *True Sexual Morality: Recovering Biblical Standards for a Culture in Crisis.* Wheaton, IL: Crossway, 2004.

Howard, Jeremy Royal, ed. *The Holman Apologetics Commentary on the Bible: The Gospels and Acts.* Nashville: B&H Publishing, 2013.

Kitchen, K. A. *On the Reliability of the Old Testament.* Grand Rapids, MI: Eerdmans, 2003.

_____. *The Bible in Its World: The Bible and Archaeology Today*. Eugene, OR: Wipf and Stock, 2004.

Levering, Matthew. *Biblical Natural Law: A Theocentric and Teleological Approach*. Oxford: Oxford University Press, 2008.

Meyer, Stephen C. *Darwin's Doubt: The Explosive Origin of Animal Life and the Case for Intelligent Design*. New York: HarperCollins, 2013.

_____. *Signature in the Cell: DNA and the Evidence for Intelligent Design*. New York: HarperCollins, 2009.

7

The Problem of Evil and Hell

Few people do not have their faith shaken from time to time by the pervasiveness of evil and suffering in our world. Nearly every Christian has met people who claim to no longer believe in God because of the apparent abundance of undeserved pain and hardship in the world. What are we to make of these kinds of complaints? The first thing we need to do is define precisely what the problem of evil is.

7.1 What is the problem of evil?

Evil can be defined in a variety of ways. A rather informal way of putting it is that evil is the bad stuff that people experience—it is any apparently undeserved suffering. Philosophers and theologians sometimes distinguish between moral evil—the bad things caused by decisions made by rational creatures—and natural evil—the bad things caused by events in the world of nature, such as earthquakes, hurricanes, diseases, and so forth. Evil is a problem for us simply because we do not want to experience it, either directly or indirectly. In the realm of religious belief, however, it takes on a more formal character, and this is what is most often meant when people speak of something called "the problem of evil."

The problem can be quite simply stated in the form of an argument: An all-good and all-powerful God, if he existed, would prevent evil from happening.

Evil, however, exists. Therefore, an all-good and all-powerful God does not exist. This is an old argument, which was known even in the ancient world. Essentially it is an argument for the non-existence of God. It is the only *a posteriori* argument that, if sound, appears able to deliver this conclusion, since it is the only argument that can point to something in the world that appears clearly at odds with God's reality. As such, it is no surprise that atheists never tire of bringing it up, especially when confronted with the positive case for theism and Christianity that we have so far been discussing. What are we to make of it? The argument is valid, in the sense that if the premises are true, the conclusion will follow. But are the premises true?

While no Bible-believing Christian would doubt the truth of the second premise, that evil exists, there seems to be no compelling reason to accept the truth of the first premise, that an all-good and all-powerful God would prevent evil from happening. Maybe he would, but perhaps he might have a good reason for not doing so. As long as such a good reason could possibly exist, the problem of evil loses its strength as a rational argument against God's existence. This of course does not mean that evil becomes unproblematic or easy for people to deal with when it occurs, but it does mean that the problem of evil cannot be utilized as conclusive evidence for the non-existence of God. It might be added that in a godless world, suffering would be even more acute since there would be no hope of final justice or restoration. Hence, if the problem of evil were a successful argument, it would actually make the experience of evil worse.

7.2 What are some possible responses to the problem of evil?

The question that naturally occurs at this point, of course, is, do we know of any plausible reasons for why God might not prevent evil? The answer is that we indeed do, but it should be pointed out that even if we did not, this would not imply that no reason could possibly exist. It would simply mean that we have not thought of one. Obviously, God's thoughts are not our thoughts and his ways are not our ways. Hence, there is no reasonable way that a person could be entirely confident that the first premise stated above is true in any case. But it is still desirable to know of some possible reasons, especially since this issue is so often cited as a reason for why people have walked away from Christianity.

One important reason should in fact be rather obvious, at least for people who know the Bible and take it seriously. Although rarely considered by skeptics, Christians know the truth that all sinners deserve punishment. Not just a little hardship or inconvenience, but everlasting punishment. Therefore no one has legitimate grounds to claim that any human being does not deserve to experience suffering. No matter how unfair it may seem to us that "good" and "decent" people suffer more than people we consider immoral, from God's point of view there are no good and decent people apart from his grace, and even after regeneration, there is no one whose deeds are perfect. The real mystery, when the problem is looked at from this angle, is not that a good God permits evil to happen but that a just God shows so much mercy and forbearance.

There is still the question, however, of why God ever allowed evil in the first place, or why he created the world knowing that it would come to be overrun with evil. Perhaps the most popular answer, which goes back to the early church, is that God permits evil in order to preserve our free will. The line of thought here is that free will would not exist if there were no possibility of choosing evil, God wants human beings to be responsible creatures who can freely choose to respond to him, and therefore he has made it possible for human beings to choose to do evil.

This may seem plausible enough on the face of it. Having free will is obviously more desirable than being coerced, and it is true that if we are to be held responsible for our actions, there must be free will in some sense. There are, however, a few objections to this idea worth noting. One is that God is free and yet has no ability to do evil. It does not seem, therefore, that freedom and the inability to choose evil are strictly opposed. Another issue is that while this theory may go some length to explain God's allowing moral evil, it does not seem to say anything about why God also chose to permit natural evil. This does not seem to be a significant difficulty, however, provided we accept the doctrine of the fall and the view that natural evils are a consequence of human sinfulness. Perhaps the most significant shortcoming of this theory is that the Bible nowhere seems to suggest that God prizes human freedom to the extent that human freedom is of greater value to him than the existence of a world without sin. Hence, this theory appears to have no real mooring in Scripture. This does not mean it is necessarily wrong, since the Bible does not reveal everything to us, but a theory that seems to have some biblical support would be preferable to one that does not seem to have any.

Another common idea, which also has roots in the early church, is that God permits evil to occur because it helps human beings to grow in character. The thought here is that many of the most valuable human virtues, such as compassion, patience, prudence, courage, and so on, could not exist without adversity or suffering. Therefore, if God wants human beings to have these precious qualities, he will have to place them in an environment where evil is a genuine possibility and these qualities can be acquired. There is much to be said for this theory. It does seem that a person with these qualities is decidedly better than someone without them, and it also seems that they could not have any real existence apart from situations in which pain and hardship were sometimes encountered. A person living in a world without evil might be perfect in some sense, and might always do the right thing, but it is difficult to see how these virtues could be genuinely possessed by such a person. Certainly they could not be exercised even if they were possessed. However, like the previous theory, this view also seems be highly speculative, for there is no statement in the Bible that asserts or suggests that God permitted the fall because he wanted humans to acquire virtues that can only exist with the experience of adversity.

Granting all this, it can be said that both of these theories have their strengths, and no doubt they both could be usefully employed in apologetic conversations. But it is not obvious that either should be a Christian's considered answer to the question of why God permits evil—for in both of these accounts, the reason God permits evil is to make possible something he wants human beings to have. In other words, both provide a human-centered account of God's willingness to permit evil. But it seems we would be on stronger ground if we were able to find an explanation that was more theocentric or God-centered. This would no doubt be a more biblical response to the problem of evil, since the Bible makes it clear that God does everything for his own glory. God's having this as his overarching purpose might strike many people today as unbecoming or selfish, but seeing its truth follows from having a proper understanding of who God is.

7.3 What is a theocentric response to the problem of evil?

Often when people do something for their own glory, or to demonstrate their character, talents, and abilities to others, we think of it as a self-centered act, or one that is immature and attention-seeking. The notion that God acts for his own glory can therefore appear in quite a negative light if we employ this same kind of thinking in his case. We will likely imagine him as a horrible narcissist, and hardly as a being worthy of our highest esteem. But a more correct view of the matter will be arrived at if we ask ourselves why it is fitting and even a duty for us to give glory to God and do things for the glory of God. The answer is that God is the greatest and most perfect being in existence. There is nothing more true, good, and beautiful than the divine essence. This is a purely objective truth about God and about reality; it is not a mere opinion. It is therefore only proper and right that all of our actions be done for his sake, and in order to bring him glory. We must, in other words, place the creator above his creatures in our thoughts, words, and deeds, for otherwise our values will be objectively disordered.

Now what is true for us is no less true for God. Because he is the pinnacle of reality, it would be wrong, foolish, and even crazy for him to act chiefly for the sake of something other than himself. He would then himself be guilty of elevating the creature above the creator, and making the lesser thing the end of his activities instead of the greater, which would be no less inappropriate in his case than it is in ours. This is why it makes sense and in fact is good to say that God does everything for his own glory. When God does this, he is only being perfectly just and thus doing what a perfect God should do.

Regarding the problem of evil, thinking in these terms about God's motives brings us to a different reason for why God permits evil than we saw in the previous two responses. A clue to what this reason is can be found in some key Scripture passages. The first comes from the story of Joseph and his brothers. As most readers no doubt know, Joseph was sold into slavery by his jealous brothers. Through a series of remarkable events, Joseph became the vizier or second-in-command to the pharaoh of Egypt. When famine struck, Joseph's brothers came to Egypt to find food. Because Joseph was in a position of authority, he was able to help them. He told his brothers, "As for you, you meant evil against me, but God meant it for good, to bring it about that many people should be kept alive, as they are today" (Gen. 50:20, ESV). The suggestion here is that God permitted evil because he was able to bring goodness out of it that would not have existed otherwise, at least not without a miraculous intervention. His permission was therefore a means by which his wisdom and kindness could be displayed.

We see essentially the same explanation being given for God's permitting a much greater evil deed in the Book of Acts. Peter was addressing a crowd of Jews during the Feast of Pentecost. The evil deed in this case was the crucifixion. The apostle told the crowd that Jesus was "delivered up according to the definite plan and foreknowledge of God" (Acts 2:23, ESV). What was God intending to accomplish by permitting this evil? His aim, of course, was the objective justification of the world, a result that could not have been reached without the death of his beloved Son. As in Genesis, God's perfect wisdom and goodness were displayed through his permission of evil.

Yet one more piece of evidence comes from Romans 11:32, where Paul writes that "God has consigned all to disobedience, that he may have mercy on all" (ESV). It appears that Paul is here affirming that all human beings were allowed to experience the consequences of original sin so that all would be able to receive God's mercy. This, indeed, is the chief way in which God's goodness and wisdom are displayed by means of his permitting evil to occur: people who in themselves are capable of nothing good are justly made heirs of everything good.

It thus seems warranted to say that this is the Bible's view of why God permits evil. It is allowed so that he and his attributes are glorified by the goodness he is able to bring forth from it. In our own lives we sometimes are unable to see why a particular evil is permitted, but it makes sense to think that what was true in the cases of Joseph and Jesus holds true for all cases in which evil occurs; in some way God is or will in the future be glorified by it. We might not have the slightest idea how, but we can have confidence that the maker of heaven and earth knows what he is doing and will do what is best. If we recognize that anything that intentionally and truly brings glory to God is by nature good, then we will understand that God is good in permitting evil if his permitting evil serves to bring glory to himself. The problem of evil therefore fails as an argument.

7.4 Can it be just for God to condemn anyone to hell for eternity? What about people who never even hear the gospel?

Closely related to the problem of evil is the problem raised for some people by the idea of hell. Once again, God's justice, fairness, and decency are at stake. The teaching that hell is real and that punishment in hell lasts for eternity is another reason often given for why people leave Christianity (at least traditional forms of it). Objections to hell typically seem to take the following forms:

1. It is unfair to punish a finite number of sins with an everlasting punishment.
2. It is unfair to punish ignorant, foolish human beings with an everlasting punishment. Those who die without ever hearing the gospel are especially deserving of mercy.
3. Punishment should always be remedial. Since an everlasting punishment could not serve that purpose, it is wrong.
4. A genuinely loving God would never subject his creatures to everlasting

punishment.

In response to the first, it is important to understand that the gravity of sin is in part determined by who is sinned against. This idea rubs many people the wrong way in our contemporary society, because we think of all people as being equal and as having equal rights under the law. However, even we can get some sense of its truth when we think about what strikes us as worse: when someone with a saintly character is cheated or swindled or when someone who is known as a miscreant is treated the same way. Most people have a sense that the former really is worse than the latter because the person with good character deserves better than the person with bad character. Now imagine what God deserves. He deserves perfect and absolute love and obedience, and therefore any falling short of such perfection on our part is a grievous sin. Because God is infinitely good, sins against him must be infinitely bad. This entails, of course, that it is in no way unjust for God to subject a sinner to endless punishment, even for what seems to us like a minor failure to keep God's law.

With regard to the second objection, it is important to remember that if humans are ignorant and foolish, that is not because God created them in such a state. They have become ignorant and foolish through the corruption caused by original sin. It must be kept in mind that from a biblical standpoint, we are not simply individuals before God. We have a corporate identity as well—being either in Adam or in Christ. No one who is in Adam is innocent of Adam's sin. Therefore, people cannot claim that their ignorance and foolishness make them innocent. They would be neither ignorant nor foolish if they were truly innocent and thus free from corruption. The same can be said for those who never hear the gospel. The fact that they have no relationship with God is not something for which they are blameless. God, moreover, has no obligation to send his gospel to any sinners. Otherwise, they would be deserving of his goodness, when the truth is that after the fall no human being deserves anything but punishment—everything we receive after the fall is the result of grace and mercy alone.

It might naturally be objected at this point that it is unfair to hold people responsible for Adam's sin and make them suffer the consequences of a corporate identity that they never chose for themselves. But the objector here seems to take for granted that he would not have likewise sinned if placed in Adam's position, and what reason does he have to believe that? It might be more correct to think that if Adam sinned with all his gifts and personal knowledge of God, then any human being placed in his position would have sinned as well. It is of course impossible for us to know for sure what we would have done in such a position, but God no doubt had knowledge of this when he created Adam. Given the possibility that we would all have fallen into sin, we should not assume that some great injustice was committed when all of Adam's posterity were implicated in his lawbreaking.

Regarding the third objection, it is simply not the case that punishment must be remedial to be good. Justice is good whenever it is truly just, and justice is simply giving a person what he or she deserves. The idea that punishment can only be good if it is remedial or restorative implicitly rejects the idea that justice *per se* can ever be good. This manner of thinking owes much more to the cultural mores of the contemporary West than it does to any self-evident moral principle.

The fourth objection is, if anything, even more a result of our culture's habits of thought than the previous one. It depends on having a picture of God as an indulgent, doting father who desperately wants to be liked by his children and therefore is happy to get whatever obedience from them he can. But of course God is not like that at all, and even to imagine that he is suggests that someone is unfamiliar with the God of the Bible and has replaced him with an idol. This objection is thus based on ignorance of who God is. God is indeed perfect love, but he is also perfect holiness and justice, and being perfect, the latter attributes are not and cannot be made subordinate to the former. If they were, God himself would not be perfect. One of the great things revealed by the cross is that God's love and justice are completely in accord, and neither is nor can ever be sacrificed to the other. People of course might not like the God of the Bible—in fact, by nature no one is disposed to like him—but that has no bearing on the truth regarding his being and character. And anyone who has achieved a modicum of spiritual maturity will recognize that a God who is all love and no justice is actually as impossible as a square circle, since one cannot truly love and yet turn a blind eye to injustice perpetrated against the objects of one's love.

Having now indicated why evil and hell present no real obstacles to Christian belief, in the next chapter we will look at a final set of objections that have arisen due in large part to the ways of thinking and prevailing attitudes that shape our contemporary world.

For Further Reading

Christensen, Scott. *What about Evil? A Defense of God's Sovereign Glory*. Phillipsburg, NJ: P&R Publishing, 2020.

Davies, Brian. *The Reality of God and the Problem of Evil*. New York: Continuum, 2006.

_____. *Thomas Aquinas on God and Evil*. Oxford: Oxford University Press, 2011.

Dembski, William A. *The End of Christianity: Finding a Good God in an Evil World*. Nashville: B&H Academic, 2009.

Evans, G. R. *Augustine on Evil*. Cambridge: Cambridge University Press, 1982.

Evans, Jeremy A. *The Problem of Evil: The Challenge to Essential Christian Beliefs*. Nashville: B&H Academic, 2013.

Geisler, Norman L. *If God, Why Evil?: A New Way to Think about the Question*. Minneapolis: Bethany House, 2011.

Jones, Clay. *Why Does God Allow Evil?: Compelling Answers for Life's Toughest Questions*. Eugene, OR: Harvest House, 2017.

8

Some Additional Objections

At this point, several of the most pressing objections to the Christian faith have been cleared away. Yet there are some additional ways in which our present context presents challenges to the Christian faith that should be mentioned. Some of these objections proceed from the basic idea that Christianity is not sufficiently "modern" or in tune with the world revealed by science and marked by human progress, and therefore it should be rejected. Others proceed from a "postmodern" view that Christianity is too absolute in its claims to be acceptable. In this chapter we will consider both of these types of objections.

8.1 Is Christianity anti-intellectual?

It became a common stereotype in the early twentieth century to imagine orthodox Christians as backwards, ignorant, stubborn, and lacking in curiosity. Because of this, many people have absorbed the idea that Christianity is not really for smart, inquisitive, or learned people. Sometimes this view is unconsciously or implicitly held even by Christians themselves. Such Christians judge that Jesus wants us to have a simple, childlike faith and that it only detracts from our spiritual life to introduce intellectual matters into it.

It is important to realize that this view finds virtually no support in the mainstream of the church's history. In fact, even now it would still be accurate to say that the majority of the great minds in human history have belonged to Christians. We need only think of people like St. Augustine, Boethius, St. Anselm, St. Bonaventure, St. Albert the Great, St. Thomas Aquinas, Duns Scotus, Luther, Melanchthon, Johann Gerhard, Kepler, Pascal, Boyle, Leibniz, Étienne Gilson, and C. S. Lewis, among many others. Given this legacy, it is a great mistake to imagine that Christianity is by nature uninterested in the life of the mind. Ironically, only those who lack a broad interest in intellectual matters are able to be ignorant enough to suppose that Christianity is naturally anti-intellectual.

Regarding the notion that our faith is to be childlike, it is true that we are to trust God as a small child trusts his father. But this does not have anything to do with being ignorant of the world or suspicious of genuine learning. Jesus' declaration that we are to love God with all our mind would seem to actually mark any such attitude as being against God's will for us.

8.2 Is Christianity an impediment to human liberation?

The modern world shows an unprecedented interest in achieving freedom from all sorts of constraints and limitations on individual behavior. This is true whether these impediments to self-expression come from traditions, laws, religious teachings, churches, families, or socioeconomic situations. Many critics of Christianity have singled out Christian beliefs about differences between the sexes and God's intentions for the gift of sexuality as being especially significant in contributing to such limitations. Another charge frequently heard is that the Christian focus on personal piety and on life after death makes Christians too indifferent to creating opportunities for the poor and marginalized. All of this entails, from the point of view of such critics, that Christianity in any traditional form must be regarded as oppressive, unhealthy, and harmful.

Of course, to view Christianity in this light, a person must already have assumed that Christianity is false and that the things Christianity values are worthless, or at least worth much less than Christianity claims they are. From a point of view that regards Christianity as true, it is apparent that Christianity is actually the only real source of liberation, for only Christianity can offer freedom from humanity's worst problems—namely sin, Satan, and death. People are really free, from a Christian point of view, not when they no longer experience any pressure to avoid doing what they want or the difficulties of economic hardships, but when they come to realize what human life was intended to be—a life devoted to glorifying God and loving one's neighbor. It is only this kind of life that brings genuine freedom from unhappiness and despair.

Furthermore, the assertion that Christianity is misguided for focusing on life eternal instead of life on earth is obviously absurd if there indeed is a life eternal. The stupid and harmful thing in that case would be to tell people not to focus on the life to come but to only concern themselves with the fleeting problems and possibilities of this present age. It would be to claim that material poverty is a greater evil than spiritual poverty, and to suggest that the poor have more pressing needs than the need to be pardoned by God. If there is an eternal life, critics of Christianity can thus be regarded as the ones who do not have things rightly prioritized.

In any case, there is nothing to the claim that Christians are indifferent to material poverty. The idea is simply laughable, given the unfathomable amount of time and money Christians have poured into material care for the needy over the centuries. Indeed, no charitable organization in the history of the world has done more to feed, clothe, and give shelter to the sick and impoverished than the Christian church. It seems that what critics really dislike is that Christians sometimes do not support plans to care for the material needs of the poor by means of wealth redistribution and government-run programs. But supporting the poor and supporting a specific method of caring for the poor are two separate things.

8.3 Is Christianity responsible for wars and violence?

It is a common canard in many places today that religion is the cause of most war and violence, and that Christianity has contributed its fair share to these things, as one sees in the examples of the Crusades or the Thirty Years' War. It must be said in response that the truth is that the vast majority of wars have been largely driven by political, economic, or cultural interests. Even the minority of wars in which religion has played a part have typically not been primarily caused by religious differences.

That being noted, it must also be pointed out that a war caused by religious differences is not necessarily unjustifiable or wrong. It all depends on the circumstances and what is at stake. Although the Crusades are often thought of as an example of unwarranted aggression on the part of Christians, the historical picture is more complicated. For one thing, it should be acknowledged that Muslim expansion from the beginning was marked by violence, and that the Holy Land in no way belonged to the Muslims by right. They themselves had taken it by force only a few centuries earlier. Another important consideration is that Muslims were in fact harming and even killing peaceful Christians who lived in and were making pilgrimages to the Holy Land. Given these factors, it seems unwarranted to claim that the Crusades were simply wrong. It is true that they were often ill-advised and poorly planned, and that reprehensible deeds were sometimes committed by the Christian forces. That can and should all be admitted. But if we consider the Crusades as wars fought for the sake of protecting fellow believers, there is nothing obviously unjustifiable about such an undertaking.

The fact that people who raise this objection are only ever able to point to a few well-worn examples, especially when it comes to religious wars that have involved Christians, is itself evidence that there is not much validity to it.

8.4 Is Christianity going to exist much longer?

A hundred years ago it was quite common for skeptics to claim that theistic religion was in decline, and that it would eventually die out as people became more enlightened in their understanding of reality. This theory is not nearly as popular as it once was, due to the fact that there are actually more people alive today who believe in God than ever before in human history. Regarding Christianity in particular, it is the case that it has experienced a steep decline in certain areas of the world, most notably in Europe. But it has seen great growth in other parts of the world, such as Africa and Asia. Due to its tremendous expansion in these areas, there can be no reasonable expectation that Christianity's days are numbered.

Of course, we should take seriously the fact that in Europe and increasingly in North America, Christianity is far from thriving. We need to seriously investigate the causes of this decline, come to grips with them, and do what we can to combat them. While it is true that ultimately the Spirit of God blows wherever he wants (John 3:8), we must also acknowledge that God has commanded us to spread the gospel and wants us to do it in the best way we can. This means that we have to be aware of our cultural context and active in doing what we can to make our context one in which the gospel can be heard and find a receptive audience. One of the reasons apologetics matters is that it can contribute, even if only slightly, to shaping our context so that it is conducive to the spreading of the message of Christ's redemption.

8.5 Is the belief that there are souls or spirits disproven by modern science?

In answering this question, it might be helpful to distinguish between science and scientism. Science is simply the use of the scientific method to test hypotheses about observable phenomena. It is a method of knowing, not a theory about what exists. Science in itself, therefore, has nothing to say about the reality of whatever cannot be directly or indirectly observed. Scientism, by contrast, is the view that only scientific knowledge can really count as knowledge at all. This means that since empirical realities are the only things studied by science, a person can only have genuine knowledge about those things which are perceptible by means of our five senses. A claim to know about anything else will be judged to be mere folly and baseless superstition. It must be said that this is more like a blind religious belief than anything that is supported by science itself. It is also inconsistent, since the assertion that only science is a pathway to knowledge is not itself in any way dictated or even supported by science.

Scientism often presupposes and goes hand in hand with a view of reality called materialism. This view originated in the ancient world, more or less disappeared for several centuries, and then came back to prominence during the Enlightenment. Materialism, simply put, is the belief that only things made of matter exist. Hence, if materialism is true, there can be no immaterial things such as souls, or angels, or God. Are there any good reasons to believe that materialism is true?

The answer to this question is an unequivocal no. The reality of human consciousness provides clear and immediate proof that immaterial realities exist. No material object is conscious, no matter how complex or remarkable it is. No computer, for example, is aware of itself or able to describe what is it like to be a computer. No machine is capable of feeling anything like curiosity, anger, longing, and so forth. But human beings are self-aware and capable of introspection. They can describe what it is like to have various experiences and emotions. Therefore, there must be more to a human being than matter alone. Moreover, thoughts and feelings do not have any of the properties that define physical objects. They themselves have no size, no shape, no color, no weight, no texture, no hardness, and so forth, though what is thought about might have all these things. My thought of the sun, for example, is no "bigger" than my thought of a water molecule. Thoughts and feelings are also capable of being about things that have no physical existence, such as love, faith, humility, gratitude, and so forth. It is hard to see how these things could exist if immaterial realities did not exist to experience and contemplate them.

All of these considerations make it clear that the difference between material and spiritual realities is real and cannot possibly be eliminated. Human minds exist in ways that human brains do not, even though they are intimately connected. Materialism is motivated by a desire to assert that whatever exists can be investigated by the natural sciences. The irony of this is that science is an intellectual pursuit driven by curiosity, and as such it would not exist if materialism were true. We therefore have more than sufficient grounds to be sure that spirits can and do exist.

8.6 Are not all religions really the same? Why should Christianity be preferred?

It has become common in our pluralistic culture to hold the view that all of the "great" religions of the world are really the same once a person gets past some superficial differences. All of them, it is said, are different pathways to the same salvation. The various founders of these religions are regarded as profound spiritual teachers who were similar enough to deserve equal respect, but different enough that all potentially have something of value to teach us.

Many people who affirm this outlook think of themselves as being open-minded and generous to people of all religions. But here, as always, we must ask the simple question, is any of this true? More than a few learned scholars have devoted careers to trying to make the case that it is. They have filled volumes making strained comparisons and downplaying differences. But the facts stand in their way at every turn, and the truth is that when Christianity is compared with other religions, it is not the case that the differences between them are found to be superficial. Rather it is the similarities that are superficial; the differences are what run deep.

The most fundamental difference is that in Christianity, salvation comes through what God does for us—Christianity in its purest form is from first to last entirely based on divine grace. This is why in Christianity alone the poor in spirit, those who comprehend their spiritual destitution and need for mercy, are those who are blessed. Other religions always claim that salvation is somehow up to us; it is the result of what human beings manage to achieve or accomplish.

Additionally, only in Christianity does God himself become incarnate in order to make salvation possible. Christianity, alone among the religions of the world, teaches that the mediator between God and humanity is himself fully human and fully divine. This is important, for only such a mediator could render satisfaction for the sins of the world. As human he can stand in our place, and as divine he can make adequate restitution.

Another significant difference is that the truth claims of Christianity are well supported by rational arguments and historical facts. No other religion has superior or even equal evidential support. With respect to all the founders of other religions, we are forced to take their word for what they teach. Only in Christianity is the teaching of the founder vouched for by an event as clearly factual as the resurrection of Jesus.

8.7 Is not truth relative to different times, places, cultures, and perspectives?

Today relativism is pervasive in our culture, and this means it tends to affect how everyone thinks, even Christians. Before the modern age, truth, goodness, and beauty were regarded, at least in the Christian West, as entirely objective qualities. Neither truth, nor goodness, nor beauty was "in the eye of the beholder," or determined by how people happened to think about them. But at the beginning of the modern period, people began to think that beauty is purely subjective. Later they began to think the same thing about morality. And in the twentieth century, it became quite common to believe that even truth is really relative to particular individuals or groups. Hence, we have people who talk about "their truth," a phrase that would have made no sense at all to someone living five hundred years ago.

Relativism is popular in part because it seems to give people greater freedom. As mentioned in a previous chapter, one of the main preoccupations of the modern world is achieving freedom from constraints. If every individual gets to believe whatever he or she wants, and each person's truth must be regarded as just as good as anyone else's truth, then this seems to really put individuals in charge—not only over their own lives, but over the meaning and significance of reality in general. Unsurprisingly, a lot of people are attracted to this kind of thinking which seems to put so much at the disposal of the individual.

The question we must again ask, as always, is whether there are there any good reasons for believing this perspective is correct or warranted. The answer is no, because this view of things is without any doubt self-contradictory. If there are no objective truths, then the statement "there are no objective truths" is not itself objectively true. And if it is not objectively true, then it is not true at all. Contrary to what some people might think, there is no meaningful sense in which truth can be subjective. What is true for one person but not true for others or with respect to reality itself is not truth but simply a false belief. It is what in more sane times would have been called a mistaken opinion. In short, since there is no way to escape the fact that to deny that there is objective truth is also to state an objective truth, the affirmation that truth is relative is obviously self-contradictory.

Hence it is clear that there must be absolute truths, or truths that are objectively true for everyone regardless of their circumstances. This does not mean that it is always easy to discover, recognize, or understand them, but it does mean that they must exist. Some people seem to believe that emphasizing the reality of objective truth is oppressive, because it makes it clear that the meaning of reality is not up to us. However, the truth is that the meaning reality has is a gift to us, in that it makes a truly meaningful and purposeful life possible. If we were really lords over what gets to count as true, good, and beautiful, we would have no real purpose, nor could we have. Everything would be a mere figment of our imaginations; every purpose or standard we set for ourselves would be one we could choose to change. We would be free from all objective constraints, but free for the sake of nothing. It stands, then, that objective truth is not only real, but a great good.

8.8 Is it not arrogant to insist that Christians alone possess the truth about God and human salvation and that Christ is the only way to salvation?

People outside the church sometimes assert that it is arrogant for Christians to insist that they know God's will and what is necessary for human salvation. This is usually tied to the claim that it is arrogant for Christians to assume that their religion is the only true one and the only one by means of which people can receive eternal life. Oftentimes such people want to believe that God saves everyone, or at least everyone who is a "good" person.

It would indeed be arrogant for a human being to insist that he or she knows these things apart from a well-attested revelation from God. But if a person's claims are simply the reiteration of what God himself has chosen to disclose, it is impossible to see how this alone could be a mark of arrogance. It is certainly possible that possessing knowledge of God's revelation could lead a person to feel prideful and better than others, but in the case of Christianity, such a result would only show that such a person's understanding of God's revelation is sorely deficient. It would not in any way support the idea that claiming to know this revelation is in itself arrogant. If anything, choosing to reject a revelation from God that is well supported by evidence because one finds it unpalatable is a sign of arrogance. For in such a case, a person is refusing to listen to God and humbly submit to his authority. This objection, therefore, can easily be turned on the objector, and with much more force.

We have now finished looking at objections to most of the fundamental beliefs of Christianity. Given what has been said in this and the preceding chapters, it should be clear that it is highly reasonable to be a Christian who holds traditional views about God, mankind, and the Bible. This is the case even though there are many things taught in the Bible that are mysterious, such as the doctrines of the Trinity and the incarnation of the Son of God. But we should be willing to accept the truth of these things because the truth of the Bible itself is strongly supported in all the ways we have seen.

Having completed our case for traditional Christianity broadly speaking, we can now turn to the question of why a Christian should be a confessional Lutheran instead of a member of some other confessional tradition. We will turn to this matter in the next chapter.

For Further Reading

Carson, D. A. *The Gagging of God: Christianity Confronts Pluralism*. Grand Rapids, MI: Zondervan, 1996.

Erickson, Millard J. *Truth or Consequences: The Promise and Perils of Postmodernism*. Downers Grove: IL: InterVarsity, 2001.

Groothuis, Douglas. *Truth Decay: Defending Christianity against the Challenges of Postmodernism*. Downers Grove, IL: InterVarsity, 2000.

Lane, Jason, et al. *The Christian Difference: An Explanation & Comparison of World Religions*. St. Louis: Concordia, 2019.

Moreland, J. P. *The Soul: How We Know It's Real and Why It Matters*. Chicago: Moody, 2014.

Schmidt, Alvin J. *How Christianity Changed the World*. Grand Rapids, MI: Zondervan, 2004.

Trueman, Carl R. *The Rise and Triumph of the Modern Self: Cultural Amnesia, Expressive Individualism, and the Road to Sexual Revolution*. Wheaton, IL: Crossway, 2020.

Veith, Gene Edward. *Post-Christian: A Guide to Contemporary Thought and Culture*. Wheaton, IL: Crossway, 2020.

Wells, David F. *Above All Earthly Pow'rs: Christ in a Postmodern World*. Grand Rapids, MI: Eerdmans, 2005.

9

Why Be Lutheran?

After someone has been led by the Holy Spirit to embrace the Christian faith, he or she is faced with a plethora of membership options with respect to confessional traditions and particular churches. Some people are satisfied with adhering to the most basic Christian beliefs and do not feel that having a well-defined doctrinal position is of great importance. Such people often think that to be a partisan for a particular tradition is to unnecessarily create division among Christians. This stance seems to be embraced by many who choose to attend non-denominational churches. While the peace-loving spirit of such people is to be commended, they often overlook important issues discussed in Scripture because they wish to avoid disagreements or taking sides in controversies. However, if God has revealed his will concerning a certain matter, we cannot choose to ignore it simply because it is understood differently by various Christian traditions. It is clear that God would not speak to us about a given topic if he really did not desire us to hold any particular views about it. We have a duty, therefore, to attempt to determine which confessional tradition is correct in interpreting Scripture taken as a whole, or which at least comes closest to being correct. In this chapter we will consider how a person might do that.

9.1 What criteria should we use to select a confessional tradition?

Many people choose a church because the people are welcoming, or the pastor is a great speaker, or because the church offers exciting programs. These are typically all good things. But anyone who knows the God of the Bible will not be able to believe that God would want us to put such things before the issue of whether or not a church affirms and teaches the truth found in his word. Truth is of the utmost importance to the Lord, and therefore it should be of the highest importance to his people. We therefore should go to a church that teaches what is true and nothing but what is true. But how can we know if a church does this?

Because we know that the Scriptures, being God's revelation to us, are entirely true, we can start to answer this question by proposing a simple rule: Whichever church is correct in its doctrine must agree fully with everything that is clearly taught in the Bible. Therefore, if something is clearly taught in God's word, but it is rejected by a church, we can be confident that the church departs from the truth with respect to that matter. Of course, we instantly face the problem that every church seems to hold that its doctrine is right, while that of other churches is in some way wrong. This might make us think the situation is hopeless. But that is not true, because we do not have to take any church's word for this. There is a way to settle who is right. We must go to the text of Scripture itself with an impartial mind, a desire to hear what God has to say to us, and a knowledge of what principles or rules are required to interpret the Bible accurately. If we do this, contrary to what some people suppose, certain positions will stand out as being the clear teaching of Scripture, and we can then begin to rule out joining churches that deny these positions.

9.2 What principles are needed to interpret the Bible correctly?

The first thing we should consider when interpreting the Bible is what the intent and purpose of its divine author was in giving it to us. It is evident enough that the Scriptures were provided so we would possess the information and guidance necessary to have a restored relationship with God. It is an eminently practical book. As such, God no doubt made it clear and unambiguous enough to serve this purpose. To provide to us with information and guidance that no one could understand, or could understand only with great difficulty, would not have been the action of a wise and good creator whose aim in giving it was to be reconciled with us. Therefore, if Christianity is true, then the Bible must be clear enough in most places to be correctly understood without great difficulty. This means that differences in interpretation will generally be the result of interpretive mistakes and not ambiguities in the text itself.

That being granted, there are a few principles we must keep in mind when reading the Bible in order to grasp the truths it contains and avoid mistakes. These principles are at least implicitly taught by the Bible itself, so it cannot be said that using them involves the imposition of foreign or unwarranted rules. One principle that will lead us to the correct reading of a passage if we apply it carefully is that we must take the text as it stands and interpret it in a literal sense unless there are clear signs that a figurative sense was intended by its author. In all language, the literal sense is the primary sense, and therefore, when interpreting anyone's words, we need to first look for what is literally meant before we can determine if the author meant for his words to be taken in some other sense. If we do not read the biblical text with this principle in mind, we will be free to impose our own meaning on the word of God, which is what people do when they resist the literal sense of a passage without justification in order to suggest some kind of figurative meaning.

A related pitfall is that people sometimes allow what they think is reasonable to dictate what the meaning of the text can be. If the literal sense of a passage seems strange or baffling to them, they determine that it must mean something else that accords more with what appears reasonable in their eyes. This inappropriate use of reason to stand in judgment over God's word is another way that people prevent God from speaking to them through it. We must never assume that what seems acceptable to our fallen and limited minds is the measure of God's truth.

Another important principle is that we must always allow Scripture to interpret Scripture. This means that we cannot affirm that a text means something that conflicts with some other clear teaching of Scripture. Likewise, if a passage taken by itself seems hard to understand, we should see if other clearer passages will help us determine its proper meaning. The Bible is always to be regarded as a whole with an entirely unified message due to the unity, perfection, and constancy of its divine author. This means that each part must always be understood as belonging to the whole, and that the true context of any given passage must be regarded as the Bible in its entirety.

A third principle that ought to be used in deciding what Scripture teaches is that all those and only those verses that truly touch on a given topic are to be used in deciding what the overall teaching of the Bible is with respect to that topic. This means that verses are not to be interpreted out of context or in a fanciful way and then either applied in formulating a doctrine that they have no bearing on or ignored when they actually are pertinent. Once again, we must follow this principle if we wish to hear what God wants to tell us and avoid imposing some false meaning on the text. We can only have pure doctrine if we keep our interpretive practices equally pure. If these principles are all applied carefully and consistently, then we will see that the Bible is not the hard book to understand that some claim it is.

9.3 What can the application of these principles tell us about biblical doctrine?

A careful employment of the principles just discussed will open up the true meaning of the Bible for us, and thereby will enable us to formulate the true doctrine of the Scriptures. What do we find after doing this? As will be demonstrated below, we learn that the central teaching of Scripture with respect to human salvation is the gospel message that we are saved by grace alone through faith alone for Christ's sake alone. The way in which this salvation is brought to us is discovered to be the means of grace, or the gospel efficaciously presented to us in word and sacrament. Though the former is the ground of our salvation, it would have no ability to affect us without the latter. Hence both must be regarded as essential.

It might be wondered what the biblical evidence is for these claims. Though in this space a comprehensive discussion is not possible, we can point to where the Bible clearly teaches these things and indicates their importance. Anyone wanting a fuller, more comprehensive exposition of the biblical evidence is invited to consult the works mentioned at the conclusion of this chapter. Regarding the doctrine that we are saved only by grace through faith on account of Christ, we find testimony for this in numerous places in both the Old and New Testaments. The fact that we are saved by grace, or unmerited favor, alone is clearly taught in Acts 15:11; Rom. 3:24, 11:6; 1 Cor. 4:7; Eph. 1:6–7, 2:5, 2:8; and 2 Tim. 1:9. The truth that we receive the gifts that Christ offers by means of faith in him is taught in Gen. 15:6; Hab. 2:4; John 3:16, 3:18, 3:36, 5:24, 6:40, 6:47, 11:25; Acts 13:19; Rom. 1:17, 3:27–28, 4:5, 5:1, 10:9; Eph. 2:8–9; Phil. 3:9; Gal. 2:16, 3:11; and Heb. 10:38. The teaching that we are forgiven only because of Christ's sacrifice for us is set forth in John 1:29; Acts 4:12, 10:43; Rom. 3:25–26, 5:9–10, 5:18; 2 Cor. 5:21; Eph. 1:7; 1 Tim. 2:5; Titus 2:14; Heb. 2:9, 9:15, 9:28, 10:14; 1 Pet. 2:24, 3:18; 1 John 2:2, 4:10; and Rev. 1:5. A study of all these passages using the interpretive principles outlined above will clearly establish that we are indeed saved solely by grace, solely through faith, and solely on account of Christ.

Sometimes it is objected that this reading of all of these passages cannot be correct because the second chapter of the Book of James states that a person cannot in fact be saved by faith alone. In particular, in James 2:24, it is expressly said that "a man is justified by works and not by faith alone." What are we to make of this? Does this overturn everything claimed so far? One thing that must be remembered is that God's word is not capable of actually teaching contrary things. Therefore, the meaning of this passage must be congruent with the large number of passages already referred to. The Lutheran commentator Paul Kretzmann helpfully asserts with respect to this chapter in James that

> the apostle here characterizes a person that has mere knowledge of the head, of the mind, concerning the facts of salvation, but is without the faith of the heart which is bound to be active in love. Real faith, saving faith, without some evidence of its presence in the heart, is unthinkable. Such faith has nothing in common with saving faith; such faith is a delusion and vanity. (*PCBNT* Vol. II, 504)

He adds that

> faith, if it has not works, is dead, being by itself. Works are a necessary concomitant, an inevitable fruit of real faith. Spurious, hypocritical faith, then, being without works, is no faith; or if one wishes to assume that there was faith at one time, it is certain that such faith has died and is no longer able to bring forth real fruit in the shape of good works. A faith by itself, without good works, is simply unthinkable. (*PCBNT* Vol. II, 505)

The right way to take this passage in James, then, is to say that though we are saved by faith alone, saving faith is never alone but is always accompanied by good works. If there are no such works, then there can be no genuine faith, and therefore works are necessary as evidence of the reality of saving faith.

Concerning the means of grace, we find ample assertions about their efficacy throughout the word of God. The power of the word to create and sustain faith in Christ is attested to in Isa. 55:11; John 6:63, 17:20, 20:31; Acts 11:14, 20:32; Rom. 10:17; 1 Cor. 2:4; Gal. 3:2; 1 Thess. 1:5, 2:13; Heb. 4:12; James 1:18; and 1 Pet. 1:23. That baptism has the power to wash away sins and produce faith and a clean heart is made clear in John 3:5; Acts 2:38, 22:16; Rom. 6:3; 1 Cor. 6:11, 12:13; Gal. 3:27; Eph. 5:26; Col. 2:12; Titus 3:5; Heb. 10:22; and 1 Pet. 3:21. The power of the Lord's Supper to strengthen faith and forgive sins on account of Christ's presence in the elements is made manifest in Matt. 26:26–28; Luke 22:19–20; and 1 Cor. 10:16, 11:27–29. Once again, if proper principles are applied in the interpretation of these passages, it will be evident that they must be taken at face value and not explained away or given some figurative reading that the text itself does not condone.

We have now established that these teachings hold a central place in the Bible. The next question is, which traditions affirm them? As will be seen in the remainder of this chapter, the doctrine of the Bible on these topics is only fully consistent with what the Lutheran church affirms in its confessions.

9.4 How are the teachings of Roman Catholicism and Eastern Orthodoxy inconsistent with biblical doctrine?

While these churches tend to preserve the power of the means mentioned above, and thus in particular grant great importance to the sacraments of baptism and communion, they deny key elements of the gracious gospel that the means are meant to convey to us. They therefore misunderstand how we are saved through them.

For the Roman Catholic Church, the gospel is more or less regarded as a new law, or a set of moral precepts taught by Christ, which by obeying we can attain a state of justification. The grace that is received through the sacraments is thus not a grace which imputes to us the all-sufficient righteousness of Christ, nor a grace that remits all sins, but an infusion of grace that enhances a person's ability to obey the gospel and thereby to earn salvation. The operating of the sacraments is therefore the power that puts salvation within someone's reach, while the gospel is the teaching that he or she is empowered to follow by means of them. It is obedience to this teaching in the form of good works that ultimately determines a person's salvation. The formula "by grace alone through faith alone for Christ's sake alone" is thus denied in Roman Catholicism because works are regarded as the deciding factor in the attainment of justification.

We can turn to the canons from the sixteenth-century Council of Trent to see clear denials of the biblical teaching that salvation is by grace alone, through faith alone, for Christ's sake alone. Faith, according to Roman Catholicism, is merely intellectual assent to what the Church of Rome teaches as being true. This being so, it is merely a precondition of justification and not that through which justification is received. As a consequence, the attaining of justification is understood by Roman Catholicism to be the result of making good use of grace by performing works that are merit-earning. Justification is thus not truly distinguishable from sanctification; it is a process in which a person progresses by the performance of works from being less justified to being more justified. However, such a person can never be certain of just how justified he or she is, so assurance of salvation is impossible without a special revelation from God.

Concerning the means of grace, the role of the word is generally quite minimal in Roman Catholicism, while the sacraments are considered to be of central importance. This is due to the fact, mentioned a moment ago, that the sacraments are considered key to enabling the pursuit of justification. Since what the sacraments grant is not forgiveness but grace in the sense of a new power to perform good works, trust in God's mercy is not considered essential to receiving their benefits. As a consequence, the sacramental theology of Rome does not hold that faith is requisite on the parts of recipients in order for the sacraments to be efficacious. Infants are therefore not granted their own personal faith through baptism, but are baptized into the faith of the Roman Catholic Church. Regarding communion, grace is received in the sense already described, but mortal sins are not forgiven. In sum, faith and forgiveness are not given the same place in Roman Catholic sacramental theology that they appear to have in Holy Scripture. This being so, although the Roman Catholic emphasis on the importance of the sacraments can be commended, their understanding of how the sacraments function should not be adopted.

Eastern Orthodoxy is similar to Roman Catholicism in some respects, but significantly different in others. The concepts typically used in Western theology (both Protestant and Roman Catholic) do not always have a prominent place or role in Orthodox theology. Moreover, the concepts used are rarely defined with the sort of rigor or exactness that is typical of Western theology. For our purposes here, it is sufficient to note that Eastern Orthodoxy does not distinguish in any notable way between justification and sanctification. For this reason, salvation is not the result of a divine declaration received by faith that one's sins are forgiven for Christ's sake alone. It is rather a process by which one grows in righteousness through one's willing participation in the sacramental life of the church and daily efforts to become godlier through prayer and other practices. By cooperating with the empowerment of divine grace in order to engage in such activities, one becomes ever more "deified" in the sense of participating more fully in God's reality. The importance given to free will and cooperation in this movement towards deification means that people are ultimately responsible for their own salvation in Eastern Orthodoxy. If we consider that Scripture attributes our salvation to God alone, and clearly teaches our profound helplessness apart from God's gracious activity, we will have to conclude that there is a serious misunderstanding of biblical truth in this church body.

9.5 How is the teaching of most Protestant traditions inconsistent with biblical doctrine?

In Protestant churches the gospel is sometimes better understood than in Roman Catholicism and Eastern Orthodoxy. This is unsurprising, since most if not all of these churches can be said to have been influenced by Lutheranism in some way. However, in these churches another problem prevails. Whereas the two bodies just examined teach that the means are efficacious but do not properly understand how they are efficacious, in Protestantism there is a tendency to not regard them as efficacious at all. As a result, many Protestants do not regard the word as having the intrinsic power to effect conversion and sustain faith, and they do not really know what to do with the sacraments, or why they are needed at all. This latter fact is especially telling, for the sacraments clearly have great importance in the Bible and were central to the life of the New Testament church. The fact that many Protestants are unable to find any significant or distinctive place for them in their theologies suggests that these Christians are failing to come to terms with what Scripture teaches.

There is, however, a wide range of sacramental views in Protestantism, so it is important not to paint with too broad a brush. In most non-denominational, Holiness, Pentecostal, and Baptist churches, very slight significance is granted to the sacraments. These churches often celebrate the Lord's Supper infrequently, and when they do, it is regarded only as presenting the participant with a symbol that should provoke reflection on Christ's death. In other words, something is supposed to happen during the Supper that could just as well occur without the sacrament. Baptism is seen as a believer's making a public statement about one's faith in Christ, but no more. As such, it is not really different from any other form of testimony given about one's faith. We can see that the theology of these churches would not be much affected if they dispensed with the sacraments altogether.

Confessional Reformed churches tend to do slightly better, in that they see participation in the Lord's Supper as strengthening the faith of believing participants and thereby promoting their sanctification. These churches do not, however, generally teach that Christ is united to the elements or that taking the Supper grants the forgiveness of sins to believers. Baptism is seen as a sign of God's covenant with believers but is not regarded as having any inherent power to grant faith and regeneration.

In Anglicanism, which of all the Protestant churches is closest to Lutheranism, higher views of the sacraments generally prevail. The understanding of the Lord's Supper found in the Thirty-nine Articles of the Church of England is essentially the same as that of the confessional Reformed churches, but many Anglicans today choose to affirm a view of this sacrament quite similar to that found in Roman Catholicism. Due to the direct influence of Lutheranism, the Anglican view of baptism as expressed in these articles is arguably the same as that found in the Augsburg Confession. Both traditions agree that baptism has the power to grant faith and regenerate recipients. It can thus be concluded that Anglicanism, in at least some of its forms, comes quite close to Lutheranism. However, even at its best, it generally falls short of complete congruity with the Scriptures, and the doctrinal latitude that is generally tolerated in Anglicanism means that it sometimes falls far short.

9.6 Is Lutheran doctrine the same as biblical doctrine?

If we turn to look at the confessional statements of Lutheranism as found in the Book of Concord, we will find that these statements are entirely consistent with what the Bible teaches about salvation and how salvation comes to us in the means of grace.

Lutheranism affirms, without any equivocation or ambiguity, that salvation is by grace alone, through faith alone, for Christ's sake alone. Anyone who reads the Book of Concord will have no doubts about this. The confessional statements in this book teach that salvation is entirely an act of God, who without any deserving on our part graciously sent his Son to die for us and creates faith in Christ by his Spirit. Because salvation is a work of God alone, and does not depend on us and our works, we can be certain that God will accept us for Christ's sake and have complete assurance that all who trust in his promises will spend eternity in the embrace of the Holy Trinity.

The biblical teaching on how salvation comes to us is also wholly affirmed by the confessions of Lutheranism, which teach clearly that all of the benefits of Christ's sacrifice are granted to us through the efficacious working of the Holy Spirit in the word and sacraments. It is to these means alone that we are to look for the building up of our faith and the forgiveness of our sins.

These assertions being granted, it is evident that only the doctrine of the Lutheran Confessions is fully consistent with the central teachings of Scripture concerning human salvation. Lutheran doctrine on these fundamental issues is simply biblical doctrine unmixed with error. This is more than a sufficient reason to belong to a Lutheran church, for Christians have an obligation to attend a church where the saving doctrine of the Bible is fully affirmed and maintained in its purity. The New Testament makes this quite clear when it commands us to adhere to and defend the doctrine of the apostles (Jude 1:3). Since Lutheranism alone does this without fail, a conscientious believer knowing the truth will wish to be a Lutheran.

For Further Reading

Bohlmann, Ralph A. *Principles of Biblical Interpretation in the Lutheran Confessions*. 2nd ed. St. Louis: Concordia, 1983.

Cooper, Jordan. *The Great Divide: A Lutheran Evaluation of Reformed Theology*. Eugene, OR: Wipf and Stock, 2015.

Engelbrecht, Edward A., ed. *The Lutheran Difference: An Explanation and Comparison of Christian Beliefs*. St. Louis: Concordia, 2014.

Gerberding, George Henry. *The Way of Salvation in the Lutheran Church*. 2nd ed. Ithaca, NY: Just and Sinner, 2020.

Koehler, Edward W.A., *A Summary of Christian Doctrine: A Popular Presentation of the Teachings of the Bible*. 3rd ed. St. Louis: Concordia, 2006.

Kolb, Robert, and Timothy J. Wengert, eds. *The Book of Concord: The Confessions of the Evangelical Lutheran Church*. Minneapolis: Fortress Press, 2000.

Preus, Daniel. *Why I Am a Lutheran: Jesus at the Center*. St. Louis: Concordia, 2004.

Thompson, Mark D. *A Clear and Present Word: The Clarity of Scripture*. Downers Grove, IL: IVP Academic, 2006.

Veith, Gene Edward. *The Spirituality of the Cross: The Way of the First Evangelicals*. 2nd ed. St. Louis: Concordia, 2010.

Walther, C. F. W. *All Glory to God*. St. Louis: Concordia, 2016.

10

Epilogue: Apologetics Is for the Gospel

We have seen in the preceding chapters of this little book that confessional Lutheran Christianity is strongly supported by a variety of arguments and facts. As a matter of fact, the complete discussion has had the effect of showing that confessional Lutheranism is actually more reasonable to believe than any other comprehensive view of reality. Not only is its belief in the truth of the Bible supported by numerous reasons, but its understanding of what the Bible teaches about human salvation is fundamentally correct.

This should give any Lutheran confidence in pursuing the real purpose for which apologetics exists, which is to share the good news of Jesus Christ with a world that is lost and in desperate need of Christ's righteousness. It is true that in performing this task, we are not able to be anything more than humble instruments in the hands of the Holy Spirit, but we can take great satisfaction in knowing that God gives us the opportunity to be used for the sake of expanding his kingdom. In truth, nothing could be a greater or more precious privilege.

Since the challenges in reaching unbelievers in the twenty-first century are greater than they have been in many centuries, but the gospel remains as important and needed as ever, Christians should be willing and eager to use any knowledge that can aid in making the truth of the gospel known. Apologetics is of great importance today because the confirmation it provides for the truth of Christianity can serve the spread of the gospel in this way. It is my wish as the author of this little book that believing readers will be encouraged by the evidence presented here to talk about the free forgiveness and new life we have in Jesus with all those who need him. For those readers who have not accepted the gift of forgiveness for Christ's sake offered in the gospel, I hope that they will consider the truth claims of the Christian faith and the great benefits that believers have in Christ. He is truly the only hope for a perishing world.

Abbreviations

ONGT Johann Gerhard, *On the Nature of God and the Trinity*, ed. Benjamin T.G. Mayes, trans. Richard J. Dinda, St. Louis: Concordia Publishing House, 2007.

PCBNT Paul E. Kretzmann, *Popular Commentary of the Bible: New Testament*, St. Louis: Concordia Publishing House, 1922.

Appendix

An Apologetic Dialogue

Here is presented a dialogue that is intended to illustrate in a concrete way how some of the arguments discussed in this book might be put into practice in everyday conversations. The characters are Frank, an older Christian, and his son David, a young adult who is no longer sure that Christianity is true. The two are having a talk one night while David is visiting his parents. At one point the discussion turns to spiritual matters.

David: Dad, to be honest, I don't really know what I believe anymore. I can't really stay on board with all that stuff you and mom believe. It doesn't make sense to me.

Frank: Do you still believe that God exists?

David: I don't know. If there were a God, why would the world be full of horrible suffering?

Frank: That's a good question. But let me ask you this. If there were no God, how did the universe get here? What made everything?

David: Maybe nothing did. Maybe it's just here and that's all there is to it.

Frank: Do you really think *that* makes sense? It seems to me that nothing in the universe is able to account for or explain itself. Nor does it seem like anything in it lasts forever. Do you really think it all just popped into existence without any reason? Do you think that the galaxies and living things and minds all just exist with no explanation?

David: Well, if there were a God, then why is the world so full of pain and disasters? Maybe there is a God, but it sure doesn't seem like he cares about what happens on earth.

Frank: That's a serious difficulty for people who believe what I do, but don't you think it's possible that God has some kind of a reason for allowing these bad things to happen?

David: Well, I don't see what it is, and I'm not sure any reason could be adequate to justify allowing the worst things that happen to occur, like genocide and child abuse.

Frank: Well, from my point of view, it's important to remember that we shouldn't expect everything God does to make sense to us. He is God after all. He knows everything, and his plans include everything, from the beginning of time to the end of the world. Just because we can't see why he would permit something doesn't mean there isn't an excellent reason.

David: It seems to me like you're basically admitting that you have no answer.

Frank: If that would require me to know why God does everything he does, then you're right, I don't have an answer. But that requirement seems highly misguided to me, and it reveals an improper perspective. We are not in a position to know what God's reasons are. We only know for sure what he tells us in his word.

David: So just give God the benefit of the doubt, is that what you're saying?

Frank: That's one way to put it. But I believe he has given me good reasons to think he is trustworthy, so it's not like I'm just hoping without any reason that he has a purpose for permitting these things. There also are some possible reasons for why God allows evil, so to assume that he doesn't have any good reason would be highly presumptuous.

David: What reasons are those?

Frank: Well, it seems clear that God wants people to be responsible, and that would require the freedom to do the wrong thing. Moreover, it seems to me that a lot of the things we value only exist because of adversity or hardship—for example, courage or compassion. I also think that anything that displays the glory of God is a good thing, and if God can bring goodness out of evil, then that displays his glory.

Adam: God would allow evil just so he can show off his glory? No offense, Dad, but that sounds ridiculous. Why would a God who behaved like that be good?

Frank: Well, God is not like you and me, Dave. If we were to do something to show off our good qualities or draw attention to ourselves, it would indicate a lack of humility. And that would be bad because we're supposed to be humble. We're just creatures after all; we come from dust and to dust we return. But God is the greatest reality there is. And for him to do something that shows his glory is only good and right, because it gives God the place and recognition he deserves.

David: Okay. But he's actually allowing people to suffer so he can display his glory. That seems really wrong to me.

Frank: Well, let me ask you this: Is any of this suffering undeserved?

David: Obviously. There are all kinds of good and innocent people who go through horrible things.

Frank: Well, let's assume for the sake of argument that the Bible is true. If the Bible is true, then no one is really good or innocent. Everyone participates in sin against God and other people, and therefore everyone deserves to suffer. I know that sounds harsh to a lot of people these days, but if the Bible is right, it certainly appears to be true.

David: Well, all that means is that the Bible is probably not true, because there are definitely good people.

Frank: Compared to what? Compared to other people, sure, but compared to God?

David: Why should God expect us to be perfect? That seems like a very high and unjustified expectation.

Frank: Do you think it would be right for him to look the other way when people are imperfect? Especially when these "imperfections" cause all the suffering that you are talking about?

David: Well, they cause some suffering, but not all. It's not like someone's sin causes a tornado that destroys a home or kills someone.

Frank: If the Bible is true, then even that suffering was caused by someone's sin, namely Adam.

David: I don't see any reason to believe that. Science has proven the Bible is full of myths.

Frank: How so?

David: We know the universe is billions of years old, and that living things gradually evolved. There's no way to make this consistent with the Bible. If God wanted people to believe the Bible, he should have made sure that it didn't contain mistakes.

Frank: There are many things to consider here. Regarding the age of the universe, the Bible never gives a specific age. Moreover, we have to make a distinction between empirical facts and interpretations of those facts. The age of the universe given by modern science is not, strictly speaking, an empirical fact but an interpretation of empirical facts. Interpretations can always be mistaken or subject to revision.

David: Okay, but I think scientists know what they're talking about.

Frank: Maybe, but the history of science is quite full of views that at one time seemed obviously correct but later were abandoned. It probably would be most wise to regard many scientific theories as provisional, especially those that cannot actually be empirically confirmed.

David: I suppose you would say the same thing applies to evolution?

Frank. Yes, but in the case of evolution I actually think the facts are against it. If you look into molecular biology and genetics, there are findings that make evolution improbable to the point of being impossible. And naturally if evolution is false, the biblical view of human origins is perhaps the only real alternative.

David: Then why does everyone act like evolution is certainly true?

Frank: Well, simply put, a lot of people are invested in thinking that naturalism, or the belief that there are no supernatural realities, is true. They want it to be true, and they want everyone to think it is true. Hence they talk about evolution as if it couldn't possibly be false, because it's the only theory naturalism has. But the truth is that there are quite a few indications that it is false.

David: Okay, maybe it's possible that the Bible doesn't really contradict the facts when it comes to creation. But this doesn't prove the Bible is completely true.

Frank. That's right. It's impossible to prove the Bible is true by examining empirical and historical data, since we don't have direct evidence for many of the things related in the Scriptures.

David: Does that mean you just have blind faith that it is true?

Frank: My conviction that it is true is a gift from the Holy Spirit. But my conviction is also supported by reasons.

David: Like what?

Frank: Well, the most impressive reason, in my view, is that Jesus clearly believed in the truth of the Bible. Since I am confident that Jesus is God incarnate, this settles the matter.

David: But how do you know Jesus is God? Because the Bible says so? That seems like circular reasoning. You believe the Bible because you believe Jesus is God, and you believe Jesus is God because you believe the Bible.

Frank: Not really. I believe the Bible is completely true because Jesus is God and Jesus taught that the Bible is completely true. But I believe Jesus is God because the New Testament writings are reliable pieces of historical evidence, and they indicate both that Jesus taught that he was divine and that he rose from the dead, which vindicates his truthfulness.

David: Who says the New Testament documents are reliable? Are there not many people who claim otherwise?

Frank: There are many such people, but they don't have good arguments.

There are excellent reasons to affirm that the New Testament is historically accurate.

David: And what would those be?

Frank: The writers knew what they were talking about. They all were closely connected to the events that they described. We know this because the early church only accepted documents as reliable that had a known connection to one of the apostles. Furthermore, the writers of these documents had no credible motive to be dishonest. There were no earthly rewards for being a Christian in the first century. It also wouldn't make sense for the apostles and their companions to collectively devote themselves to spreading a message that they knew had no foundation in the facts.

David: Okay. Let me get this straight. You affirm the complete truth of the Bible because you affirm the complete truthfulness of Jesus, and you affirm the complete truthfulness of Jesus because you affirm the resurrection, and you affirm the resurrection because you believe the apostles, and you believe the apostles because they had no motive to lie?

Frank: Yes, that's all correct.

David: I'll grant that this reasoning seems to make sense. But what if Christianity is harmful? Wouldn't it then be bad if it were true?

Frank: Harmful in what way?

David: Well, if Christianity is true, then it seems like most people will go to hell, right?

Frank: I won't speculate about how many will or will not, but some will, yes.

David: How could Christianity be good news if it means that some people are sent to hell merely for not being Christian?

Frank: I wouldn't characterize it that way. They don't get sent to hell simply for not belonging to a particular religion. They go to hell because they are sinners and that is what is just. Is justice ever a bad thing?

David: No, but how is it just? There are a lot of people who are not Christian who are pretty good. How can they be deserving of eternal punishment?

Frank: Well, disobeying God is not a small matter, Dave, and everyone disobeys God. A sin against an infinitely good and absolutely authoritative being is wrong to an infinite degree. As such, it rightly carries an infinite penalty. It's also not the case in my view that there are a lot of good people. As I asked before, good compared to whom? To murderers, robbers, or abusers? Or to God? People might be very good compared to the worst human beings, but all are very wicked compared to God.

David: Still, it seems like if God is loving and merciful, he wouldn't send anyone to hell for eternity, even if they appeared to deserve it.

Frank: Well, if hell is what they deserve, is God bad for sending them there? Like I said, is justice ever a bad thing? In any case, no one has to go to hell. God has provided a way to escape condemnation. What people dislike is that they can't choose their own way to escape it. They want forgiveness apart from Christ and the working of the Spirit. But there is no such forgiveness, because only Christ's perfect righteousness and atoning death can suffice to cover our sins, and faith in Christ always involves new life in the Spirit.

David: How does it make sense to say someone can die for someone else? Isn't that obviously unfair to the person who dies, and doesn't that mean that people get what they don't deserve?

Frank: How this works is somewhat mysterious, but I think you need to remember that Christians are members of Christ. They are his people, but this goes beyond just having some external connection to him. They are members of his body. He is in them, and they are in him. What they do in some sense belongs to him, and what he does belongs to them. Martin Luther called this the joyous exchange, and compared it to a poor, miserable bride marrying a noble and wealthy groom. The bride and the groom, once united in matrimony, share everything, and so it is with Christ and believers. To put it in more everyday terms, it's like Jesus is the captain of a team, and all believers are his teammates. The great things he does benefit everyone else on the team, while the bad things they do are his burden to bear. Because it is a team, however, no one can say that this is unfair.

David: Okay. You have given me a lot to think about. I'm starting to see how this all makes sense to you, though I still find a lot of it hard to swallow.

Frank: I hope you do give it some thought. If you have more questions or want to talk about this again, I'm always here.

David: Thanks, Dad.

Made in the USA
Columbia, SC
05 July 2022